How Soon

Can You

Get Here,

Doc?

By David Wynia DVM

ABOUT THE AUTHOR

Dr. Wynia has practiced Veterinary Medicine on the great plains of South Dakota for 33 years. His stories have appeared in several national and regional publications including "Bison World" and "South Dakota Magazine." His motto is "I will treat anything that isn't human." Needless to say this attitude has gotten him into some rather strange situations over the years. Writing about his experiences with humor and warmth, he will make you laugh a lot and maybe even cry a little in this heart warming collection of short stories.

Dedication

To every furry friend that ever kicked,
bit, clawed, stomped, trampled, yowled. or
otherwise showed your displeasure as we
vaccinated, dehorned, castrated, operated
on, palpated, trimmed, ear tagged, ear
notched, bled, splinted, or in any other
way made your life miserable, I dedicate
this book. May your future always filled with
restful green pastures, cool water, full feed
bunks, and mild winters. May you always
live where there are no confinement units,
needles, ropes, collars, ear tags, calf pullers,
syringes, balling guns, dehorners, knives,
pickup trucks, or any other instruments
designed by humans to make your life
more productive.

Acknowledgements

Special thanks to Elizabeth, my wife, who was invaluable in the writings and editing of this project. Without her help and guidance this book would still be only a dream.

Thanks also to David Kent, our computer wizard who made it work.

To the rest of my family and friends who gave me the courage to believe in myself.

Introduction
(An Ordinary Day)

My feet felt like two lumps of ice as I slipped into bed at 3 a.m. I knew from past experience that I could find some easy warmth for the poor buggers if I carefully and slowly eased them over to my wife's warm side. Not tonight, her reaction was quick and left no doubt where she stood.

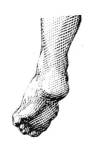

"Get your stupid cold feet off my property before I remove them and their owner to the couch and make it quick, Buster!"

I knew my best bet was to change the subject.

"Boy, did I ever have a tough one tonight. I could write a book, if I ever had any spare time."

"Yeah, and I could become the next Miss America and sing the National Anthem at the Super Bowl."

"Oh, yeah, Miss smarty pants. I'll show you one of these days. You just wait and see."

It just so happened the day did arrive quicker than I had expected and I found myself with a little time on my hands.

Like any other habitually over-worked veterinarian, I find it extremely difficult to admit even to myself, far less the general populace, that I might have free time - time to simply sit around and think of matters which do not pertain to the elimination of disease and pestilence in that small section of South Dakota I claim for my practice area. Before you jump to the conclusion that I am a complete slough off, unfit to be called "Doc," perhaps I should explain how a South Dakota mixed animal vet could find himself temporarily unyoked on a Wednesday afternoon in December.

It all started with a visit to Harry Peterson's humble farm. Fifty cows to pregnancy test, starting at 2 p.m. "How hard could it be?" I thought. "Worst case, twenty five cows an hour, done at 4 p.m., home with scotch in hand at 5 p.m." What fools we can be when we strive to deceive our own minds with wishful thinking! You see I knew better from several other visits to this little house on the prairie. You know the place, the fences consist of a few bent steel posts held up by a rambling strand of electrified barbed wire which miraculously manages to contain all manner of Holstein-cross cattle mixed in a continuous near death experience. The sway-back barn has the look of an old collie dog who has just tangled with a fifteen pound tomcat who was mad at one of his feline lady friends for her nocturnal habits. A few gaunt looking sheep and several dozen razorback porcine grazing in the feed bunk round out this quiet pastoral scene.

Just to show you how far out in left field my awareness was that eventful day, I was actually whistling a Christmas tune as the first cow hit the chute right on time at 2:10 p.m. The Christmas tune had changed to Country Western at 2:32 p.m. when the second cow submitted itself for processing and had become a slow moan at 2:46 p.m. when the third cow obediently stuck her ten inch antlers through my portable bovine head catcher.

After the third cow, things really slowed down. In fact it seemed I had been abandoned when from inside the barn there arose a clatter of boards breaking, farmers cursing and cows stridently objecting.

And then the inevitable, "I think your coveralls are scaring them, Doc. They sure never acted like this before."

Followed by, "Hey Doc, there's two of them in the haymow. What's you gonna do?"

"There is a merciful God; this will end," I foolishly chanted in my now numbed mind as that brood mare of a barn slowly released each cow to feel my cold plastic sleeve. I counted down like an Apollo astronaut in an attempt to busy my deadening cerebrum, 34 cow..33 cow.....32 cow...31 cow......30 cow..etc., etc. Eventually the sun settled behind the tree belt and the temperature dropped below zero.

"Only about ten to go. Surely there can't be more than that?"

Disaster, a giant red cow with fire in her eye and visions of dead veterinarians dancing in her head came over the top, or I should say tried to come over the top, if only she would have made it. For several long seconds she hung half out and half in, then "KAWUMP," the law of gravity claimed her posterior half. Over backwards she fell. With four hooves paddling the air, she lay in the alley stuck tight.

And then the inevitable, "What's you gonna do now, Doc?"

And the ever popular, "Hope you don't have too many other bunches today."

And of course, "You're gonna need a flashlight if you don't hurry up a little."

After several fence post pries, much swearing and two pints of schnapps, it was decided by one and all we had to get the loader and hoist her out of there.

"You'll have to wait a minute. The loader tractor is over at the Johnson place, but we'll run over and git it," was Mister Peterson's easy solution. All this as the moon poked its yellow face over the top of the hog house and a brisk south wind found its way around the barbed wire fence I was using for a wind break.

"Oh, by the way. Would you mind if we borrowed your pickup battery for a minute? I'm afraid the loader tractor battery got left in the combine."

So there I stood, eight below zero, south wind steady at 10 m.p.h. with gusts to 25, no battery to start my truck for warmth, schnapps all gone, ten cows to go, wife gonna be mad cause this was bridge night, cow in the chute starting to bloat, feet so cold I'm not sure they're still connected, and to top it off, my boots hadn't moved for so long Peterson's dog decided they had become a permanent fixture in his territory and must be marked accordingly. There I stood with all this free time on my hands and this great idea popped into my head, "I could start writing my book!"

True to my motto, "It's never too cold if opportunity is knocking" I grabbed an empty vaccine box and a broken yellow pencil from the ashtray. Before my mind could block this wonderful experience from the conscious level, I wrote down these notes on the hood of my faithful Chevy. One thing led to another and eventually the book you're reading came into being. These stories are all based on true experiences but I have taken some liberty in adding little touches to round out each happening into a more interesting episode. If you wonder which event really happened and which is added flair, just remember, the stranger it seems the more likely it is to be the complete truth.

If you're wondering, I did get home that memorable night and the final words from Mr. Peterson still warm my heart with their sincerity.

"It sure went a lot better this year, Doc. Last year we had old Doc Feeney do the cows and you know he's just too slow to make a good vet."

It Takes A Little Luck

I am always surprised by the strange misconceptions that most urban dwellers seem to have about cows. Somewhere many years ago an influential person made a preposterous observation that somehow became gospel. He observed that cows are docile, placid beasts. Maybe the little brown Jersey cows that live in New England are somewhat mellow but the near feral old range cows that live out on the prairie, for the most part, lack all social graces.

Most cows spend their days ruminating on two things:

1. How can I get out of this enclosure? (makes no difference how big the enclosure is.)

2. What else can I possibly do to make sure the next visit by the local vet can become the worst experience of his life? Believe me these are the only two things that go through the grey matter of any bovine type animal.

I like just about every cow I get to meet, they have their own way of looking at the world. I have known many cows over the years but one of my most memorable friends was a big old rangy red Angus cross cow named, quite appropriately, "Lucky".

In her prime Lucky weighed about 1400 lbs., had a pure red coat, two highly polished horns about eight inches long and two of the biggest, softest, most innocent brown eyes you would ever hope to see. Many people may not believe this but Lucky could quite definitely reason on par with your typical college sophomore.

Our relationship started on a cold winter night with that ungodly babble all veterinarians have grown to hate, the sound of a farmer's voice on the phone at 2 a.m.

"I have a cow having a little trouble calving, Doc. Think you could come right out?"

17

Even though you want to scream and curse, somehow you always manage to mumble about the same answer.

"Sure thing, Sam. I'll be right out".

And so it was I met Lucky. No, it wasn't Lucky having trouble calving, it was Lucky having trouble being born; how else could the life of such a contrary critter start?

I could see this would be a nasty one. The only thing showing was a little tail and the calf's rump part-way out. The rear legs where trying to come out first but they had turned forward so the hooves were up by his front shoulders. These breeches can be tough. You must push the calf back inside and get the two hind legs coming, then pull the little bugger out backwards, all the time the old cow will be pushing to expel this strange mass in her pelvis. Believe me that old cow can push a heck of a lot harder than the unfortunate mortal who is struggling against her.

So it began, I would push little Lucky's rump back one inch and mother would respond with a two inch push, back and forth, back and forth with me always being the loser. Time to rest and try another tactic: Stretch the cows legs straight out behind and she can't push nearly as hard, or a spinal might work but it makes the calf a lot harder to pull once you do get him straightened out.

The only thing good about these late night sojourns to deliver calves is the running commentary from the farmer. One of my favorite pieces of advice that always seems to come at the first rest stop is this:

"Why don't you just push him in and turn him around, Doc. That's what old John McCregor used to do all the time. He wasn't an educated vet mind you but he sure could snake a calf out of a cow in a hurry."

How can you tell someone that it is physically impossible to turn a calf end for end inside a cow when he is convinced otherwise? Why would you try? So my answer always seemed to come out something like,

"Well you see, Sam, I justmmm domnmmm smmmm to do you know. Well I better get back at it."

Just as I leaned down to once again try the old push, push technique the strangest thing happened. My new mother gave a heave and out popped little Lucky with her legs still pointing forward.

"Holy cow!" I exclaimed, "That's impossible."

"Don't look that way to me, Doc," is Sam's quick retort, "You're not going to charge me for a calf pull when she just had him by herself are you?"

Ignoring this obviously ridiculous statement, I answered, "That's the Luckiest calf I ever saw Sam. You better call her Lucky."

Just as I finished Christening the little snot, she suddenly gave a jump to try and stand and managed to give me a good crack in the shin with her already strong little hoof.

"Bugger, she can kick already, Sam."

"Yeah, she's a keeper ain't she, Doc?"

I never saw Lucky all summer and had pretty well forgotten the whole affair until it was time to vaccinate for bangs in the fall and I ended up out at Sam's humble farm again. Things were going as smoothly as possible with a calf going through about every minute or so, when suddenly "KAWUMP" a red tornado hit the chute and proceeded to turn herself inside out.

"Hey, Doc," hollered Sam, "remember Lucky? She's a fighter that one."

The words were no more then out of his mouth when one of those moments we all dread slowly unfolded. The red heifer somehow managed to stick one front leg under the head gate and wedged it tight between two steel cross bars. It was like slow motion as the leg slowly bent into an impossible angle, but she still wouldn't stop fighting. Guess you can't blame her too much though.

An hour later Lucky was starting to raise her head as the anesthetic wore off. Within a few more minutes she was already trying to stand on her pure white shiny new cast which still needed a little time to dry.

"She's a tough one, Doc. She'll be OK," was Sam's sunny outlook.

"Maybe so, Sam, but you better get your chute fixed or we might not be so fortunate next time."

With that Lucky gave a heave and was standing although rather unsteady. Still worried I leaned over and looked into her eyes, just to check and see if she really was back in the real world. "KERWUMP," she caught me head on with her now three inch horns, 500 pounds of stomping Lucky passed over me like a freight train. I personally counted eight kicks as she drove me into the ground but my wife swore there were at least twelve black and blue spots shaped like little cloven hooves on various parts of my anatomy.

"Did you see that, Doc?" was Sam's inane question as I picked myself up. "She's a keeper, don't you think?"

"Sam," I managed to mumble, "You would have to be an idiot to even think of keeping that rip for a cow."

"Yeah but, she'd sure make a good mother. Coyotes would never take a calf of hers."

I had several other run-ins with Lucky over the next few months. A near stomping when I removed the cast six weeks later, a little case of bloat in February when she tried to eat my left index as I struggled to pass a stomach tube to save her life, a bout with pneumonia in the early spring when she kicked me so hard my teeth rattled as I saved her life for the fourth time and several stitches in her rear leg when she took out a barbed wire fence while trying to have a meaningful relationship with the neighbor's Simmental bull. You couldn't really blame her, though, he was a rather handsome brute as bulls go.

This relationship was what got Lucky into the biggest predicament of her young life. Young heifers and Simmental bulls have a problem making babies that are much too large for these teenagers to just lay down and push out.

The phone rang at 2 a.m.

"Hey doc. I've got a heifer calving and it looks like she may need some help." It was Sam's rather sheepish voice.

I was immediately suspicious,

"Sam, tell me it isn't Lucky, please."

"'Fraid it is, Doc."

"Sam, I've told you 20 times not to keep that little bugger. Now look what you've got."

"Yeah, guess you were right, Doc. How long will you be getting here?"

Things were going pretty good until I got into the barn. Lucky seemed to have most of the steam out of her system as she stood in one corner eyeing me with her big brown eyes. Looks can be deceiving. As I busied myself getting ready with my calf pulling paraphernalia, my bucket and soap, calf puller, obstetrical suit and rope, Sam went

into action behind my back. The first I realized anything was amiss was when Sam hollered,

"Look out Doc."

Quickly turning, I saw the problem, Sam had roped the heifer but had only managed to get a short rap around the post. Here came Lucky on the end of thirty feet of lariat bucking and cursing as she made her arc. It was as if the centrifugal force speeded her flight far beyond any mortal cow's ability to run. I was right at the end of that arc.

For the second time in our quirky relationship I felt the full impact of Lucky's four hooves beating a tattoo on my body. I distinctly remembered getting kicked fourteen times as Lucky passed over me but my wife swears she could count at least sixteen black and blue hoof marks this time around. It was the fifth time I saved Lucky's life but she didn't seem to have much gratitude. As I closed up the incision from the Caesarian, I observed as much to Sam.

"She's a tough one, Doc. I'll bet this little guy you got out would make a good herd bull someday too."

"Sam," I said, "don't even think about it."

As the years went by Lucky and I developed a certain understanding. She would kick, butt, bite and scratch at every opportunity and I would cuss, yell and cry every time she got me. Pregnancy test time, Lucky would nail me; vaccination time, Lucky would really nail me; calving time, don't even think of getting out of your pickup after Lucky calved. She'd nail you so fast you'd think a mountain lion had snuck up behind you.

Fifteen years Lucky and I were at each other's throats. This time the phone call came on one of those winter mornings when the temperature was hovering around 30 below.

"Can you come out this morning, Doc? Lucky's down and doesn't seem to want to get up. I can't imagine what's wrong," was Sam's plea on the other end of the line.

"Sam," I said, "How many times have I told you to get those old cows with no teeth culled out in the fall? They always cause trouble when we have a cold winter."

"Yeah, guess you were right, Doc. How soon can you be here?"

The exam didn't take long. An old cow with no teeth can run out of energy before the owner realizes he has a problem. It wasn't really Sam's fault. As I examined her teeth or lack thereof, Lucky just couldn't resist one last crack at me. With a burst of energy she hooked me a good one with her left horn and sent me rolling one

final time into the straw. As I lay there cussing the old rip, I looked her straight in the eyes and I swear she laughed her good natured cow laugh and spoke just to me.

"One last time, Doc."

With that Lucky gently laid her head down and died.

I had to leave fast that day, I wouldn't want Sam to see the shine in my eyes even if the cold did cause it.

Friends

The first time I saw Odie, he had already de-cided he didn't particularly like me. His upper lip curved up to show two shiny, white eyeteeth and a snarl fit for a lion wandered up from his tiny lungs. Odie was one of  my most unwelcome patients - a Rat Terrier. I knew this could get nasty, Rats, Dachshunds, and Chihuahuas are the most likely trouble-makers that ever cross your table. What they lack in size, they usually make up for in belligerence. With their attitude and bellicosity they often can intimidate even the most seasoned veterinarians. Odie, as I was soon to find out, was the prototype of all nasty little dogs. All we needed was a rabies shot. Surely two grown men could handle one little dog weighing all of 8 pounds. Odie didn't think so.

Tom Joyce was the owner and he loved Odie. "The man must be deranged," was my first impression, only Odie's mother and she would have doubts, I'm sure. Tom himself just didn't fit the profile of a Rat owner. He was a large barrel-chested fellow weighing in around 300 and standing well over six foot. The truth was they made a ridiculous looking pair. As they came walking into the exam room, I thought it strange he wasn't carrying the little guy but had him running along-side, Odie barely came up to his boot and you could worry about him getting stepped on and squashed like a bug on a windshield. I soon learned it would take a bigger man than either of these two to squash Odie.

"Would you put the little guy on the table and we'll have a look?" was my simple request to start the nightmare.

"Are you kidding?" Tom replied, "I don't want to get bit."

"A bit feisty is he?" I asked, as my mind started to formulate a plan. "Surely, he wouldn't bite you just for picking him up, would he?"

"I'm afraid he would," was the rather sheepish reply. This shouldn't be so hard. I'd handle the little bugger just like a mean cat, wrap him up in a blanket and then just expose the area I needed to do the job.

"Odie must have got up on the wrong side of his basket this morning 'cause he's been surly ever since breakfast. I wish I wouldn't have told him we were going to the vet. That's when he really got owley," was Tom's weak attempt at putting a little humor into my day.

Odie immediately saw through my plan to corner him under the blanket. He could reason as well as my hired man — even under duress. Quick as a flash he backed into the corner and sat up on his rump so he had his front paws and his head to throw the blanket off as quick as I could attempt to toss it over him. After the first try he just knew that if he screamed hard enough, some nice soul from the humane society was bound to hear that he was being treated far beyond the bounds of human decency and come to his rescue. It's hard to understand how such a little set of vocal cords could make such a racket; plus the sound was so high pitched it practically tore your ear off with each shriek.

Odie, being the smart little dog he was, now decided it was time to reverse roles and go on the attack. Never stopping his screaming even for a second, he grabbed my pant cuff and proceeded to shake me like a dead calf, if you can imagine an 8 pound predator working over a 200 pound calf. It was all a little funny until the little snot reached for a better grip and included my ankle in his morsel.

"Look out, Doc. You really upset the little bugger," was Tom's contribution to the problem as he exited the exam room.

Not to be outdone, I followed at the first opportunity. It was time to rethink this entire situation. Things like hog holders, baseball bats, 12 gauge shotguns, and mortars went through my mind as I paused beside Tom in the hall.

"He doesn't seem to like to get touched," was my comment after I'd caught my breath.

"Yeah, sometimes the miss'us can touch him if he's in a really good mood, but she usually ends up with a nip before it's over."

"Really?" This was indeed strange. "You mean no one can even pet him at home? Why in the world would you want to own such an animal anyway?"

"What are you talking about, Doc. That little dog is just like a kid to us, we wouldn't think of getting rid of him." He was a little indignant that I would even think of such a thing.

"Well, I'm afraid I'll have to really get tough and use full restraint on poor little Odie. I sure don't want to get nipped anymore than I already have. You sure he needs his shot that bad?"

"Yeah, you better do whatever you have to. The way he bites we can't take a chance on him getting the rabies. I'll just stay in the hall so I don't have to watch. I don't want him mad at me over this deal." Tom was very helpful.

This time I entered the room prepared; with heavy leather gloves in place and a snare, just in case. Odie was ready, and he figured the best defense was a good offense. We met in the center of the room with the outcome very much in doubt for the first several minutes. My secretary claimed they could hear the ruckus clear down at the bank on Main Street. I doubt if this was true, six blocks is a long way. She maybe was right though. She had found an excuse to make herself scarce when the ruckus started. She figures the bank is a safe hiding place whenever the going gets a little tough and her help might be required.

Odie won a couple of battles but I eventually won the war.

"Maybe next time you could bring him on a leash. It sure makes things a lot easier," was my comment to Tom as he prepared to leave.

"You must be kidding, right?" he retorted as he went out the door with a smile on his face and Odie obediently snarling and growling alongside.

As time went by Odie and I developed a love – hate sort of relationship: we hated to see each other and loved to see the encounter come to an end. Tom was the local auctioneer in the community, so I would see him quite often up on his portable auction block on the back of his pickup. I love auction sales and rarely miss a good one unless it's calving season. Next to Tom sat his ever faithful companion Odie, on his own stool, watching the crowd, hoping, I suppose, for some poor soul to venture too close so he could take a bite or two. I swear that little dog learned my name. Whenever I arrived at the auction, Tom just to have a little fun would announce to the crowd,

"Hey look, Odie, Doc finally got here."

Odie would immediately come unhinged much to the delight of the spectators. As if that wasn't enough, at least two or three times during the sale Tom would have to throw in a comment just to liven things up a little and keep the crowd interested. He would make a remark like.

"Odie, would you like a bite out of Doc?" or, "Hey Odie, I think Doc wants to neuter you. What do you think?"

Odie, right on cue would pick me out of the throng with his eyes, growl for a few seconds, and then let out the most God-awful combination of barking and screaming you can imagine. The crowd always loved it. I, on the other hand, would shuffle my feet a little and try to look bored. Needless to say this did not make good advertising for my bedside manner. Many times I secretly longed to strangle those two.

I'd known Odie for several years when our relationship made a dramatic and strange turn around. It started one evening when the phone rang just as I was sitting down for dinner. A very distraught auctioneer was on the other end.

"Doc, it's Odie. He's been hurt bad. Can I bring him right down?"

"Yes, of course, what happened? Did he get hit by a car?" I asked even as the misgivings went through my mind. This could be grim.

"Worse than that. I'll tell you all about it when we get there."

An 8 pound dog. Worse than a car accident? All kinds of interesting speculations went through my head as I drove to the clinic.

Tom told me the story as I opened the door. He was right. It was gruesome.

"You see we were coming home from a sale over by Lake City. He was riding on my lap like always with his head out the window smelling the wind when it happened. This semi truck met us doing about 80 and Odie just sucked out. I never had a chance to grab him or anything.  It just happened too fast." Close to tears he went on, "I had to search for nearly half an hour just to find him in the ditch. What do you think, Doc?"

By this time I had the box he was in open and was looking at the sorry little animal before me. All thoughts of any animosity between us were immediately erased. This little guy needed help and a lot of it.

The trauma was unbelievable. One entire side had scraped on the asphalt, a black streak of tar covered the little guy from his ear all the way back to the tail. One back leg stuck out at an impossible angle and his breathing was barely discernible. It was hard to imagine how life could still cling to such a sorry looking bundle of flesh.

"You better just leave him, Tom. I'll do what I can but it doesn't look good." I was trying to prepare him for what looked like the inevitable.

"I don't know, Doc. I wonder if we shouldn't just put him down. I sure don't want to see him suffer."

I just hate it when people use this excuse to justify euthanasia. Of course he's going to suffer for awhile, so would a human who had been hurt. But would you rather suffer for a while or be put to death?

Usually I come back with this thought head-on and most people understand. Animals probably have their own thoughts on the matter and I bet I know which option they would choose.

"I think we should give him a chance, Tom. He's a tough little guy and a few days of pain is better then being dead, don't you think?"

"I suppose so but there's another problem, Doc. I don't have any money."

Several times I have had people come right out and state the real problem as Tom did and it sure is refreshing. I have a standard answer.

"That's OK, Tom. We'll work something out. I'll do what I can and we'll worry about the money later. Maybe we can trade for some junk you get stuck with at an auction."

The idea seemed like a good one to Tom. Junk was easy to come by in his business.

For an hour I picked little rocks, tar and debris out of Odie's burned up skin. There really wasn't much left under the trauma. His entire side needed a skin graft, but I did the best I could. After setting the broken leg and getting him as stable as possible, I spent another half an hour gently touching the broken body and sending it my energy. Does touching help? I think so, but the rest was up to him. Sometimes animals have the will to live so strong that it seems like nothing can do them in. Odie was one of these animals.

The next morning it was obvious immediately that Odie's attitude toward me had changed: no growling, no biting, just a very gentle lick as I reached in to rearrange his little body and try to make him more comfortable. For two days he lay there, eating from my hand and drinking water when I held him up. By the third day it started to look a little more promising. He would actually hold his head up alone and even tried to stand a little.

By the fourth morning he was alert and aware of the world. His first comment was, "I almost caught that stupid semi and he's mighty lucky I didn't."

Whenever I went to auction sales after that, Odie would seem to be watching for me. When I arrived, his little tail would start going a hundred miles an hour and his entire body would wiggle a greeting. Nothing Tom said would get a rise out of him. Odie and I were friends.

Greenhorns Are Vets Too

Practicing veterinary medicine on the northern great plains might be considered the worst job possible by urban standards. On the other hand it does have its moments. When I first graduated from professional school back in the sixties, I went to work in an old established practice. It had been around all of five years when I showed up. The man I went to work for, Delvin Holt, D.V.M. was six years my senior and seemed to know all there was to know. How many times I won-

dered if I would ever get to the point I could actually arrive on a farm without that knotted up feeling in my stomach. How would I screw up this one? Being a new graduate was tough. All this knowledge had been shoved into you without a lick of common sense added for flavoring.

During those first few months and years out of school it seemed as if everything that could go wrong did go wrong plus everything that went right ended up going wrong later or when it had another chance. It was a stressful time. Cows that should have died always did; cows that should have lived, died. Cows that did live usually died several days later after they had thought it through. I was lucky to have an experienced boss. Dr. Holt always helped me see the humor in learning the ropes.

"Doc," he used to say, "just remember you can't save them all, but one once in a while wouldn't hurt."

That guy could be a real confidence builder.

It amazes me how I could talk my way out of dumb mistakes without batting an eyelash. I guess desperation will make your mind do wondrous things. The first two horses I attempted to castrate both turned into complete wrecks, and the strange part is it was something I had actually done in school. In fact I had castrated at least two stallions before I ever graduated. When it came to castrating, I was a blooming expert. At that time we could only use a muscle relaxant on horses for castration. We never had a good short-term anesthetic. Problem was the relaxant only held the horse down for about three minutes. Just try and castrate a horse in three minutes when you've only done two or three in your life. It's quite a challenge.

My first horse was a little two-year-old stud weighing about nine hundred pounds, black as coal with four white stockings and pretty as a picture. I was as nervous as a rabbit in a pack of coyotes as I slipped the shot into the vein and prepared for the worst. I knew I really had to hurry, and hurry I did. Everything went great until I was done, then disaster hit. Just as I was standing clear with both testicles out and feeling very proud of myself, a little tiny piece of intestine popped out of the incision. He had a hernia and I had missed it. Within thirty seconds the pile of intestines had enlarged to the size of a bushel basket and the horse was ready to get up. I had to euthanise that poor colt on the spot and have  never really gotten over it. Even today whenever I castrate a colt I see that terrible pile of intestines laying in the straw and get that awful feeling all over again.

My second colt the mistake was just as dumb but it turned out a lot better for everyone involved. It happened a couple of weeks later and this time I was really nervous. Down went the colt and swipe went my scalpel. I had to hurry. In seconds I was really sweating as I hurried as fast as possible, got to get this done before he gets up. The problem was I couldn't find the testicles. I knew they were there. I had felt them before I put him down. What the devil was going on? Search as hard as I could they just weren't there. The horse was starting to struggle a little. Time was running out. Then I saw my mistake. Talk about a boner, in my hurry I had made my incision about four inches behind the scrotum. I couldn't find the testicles because I was doing surgery on the wrong part of the horse! My desperation invented a story just like that.

"I'm afraid the testicles aren't completely down yet and we'll have to wait a while before we can finish the job." I explained to the farmer.

You see I couldn't knock him down again and redo it because my boner of an incision was close enough to the scrotum so I would have had an incision about eighteen inches long in that poor horse. Believe it or not the farmer bought my story. I came back about a month later and did the job right. To this day that poor horse and his owner have no idea I'd done anything out of the ordinary.

As time went by things slowly started to fall into place until the time came when I started to feel like I at least knew what I was doing most of the time. Then I had my first tough rectal prolapse. It wasn't that I hadn't done one before or that I didn't know how. I just hadn't done a tough one and boy this one was a bugger.

Rectal prolapses happen to all species but mostly occur in cattle. What happens is the lining of the large bowel starts to telescope together inside the cow. This in turn causes her to strain which makes it telescope more which makes her to strain more. Eventually the whole mess is pushed to the outside where it hangs out about six to ten inches. If caught early on, they can be repaired quite easily by just turning them back inside out while you push them back into the cow, then suturing around the opening with a circular stitch so it can't come back out, really quite simple. The problems start when the owner hasn't checked his cows for a week or so and the prolapse has had several days to dry out and grow together. They then become hard as a rock.

This particular day I was really in a good mood. Things were going great. My first spay looked like it was going to live. My first equine colic was getting better. What more could a young vet ask for? Life was good. As I pulled into the yard, things got even better. I saw a note tacked to the fence and the cow standing waiting. The note told me to just take care of the cow and then turn her out to pasture. Things were always easier when the farmer wasn't home to watch. I quickly caught the old cow in the head gate and gave her an epidural, even that went well much to my relief I had been having trouble hitting the vertebrae properly but this time it worked perfectly. The first hint of trouble came when I grabbed the prolapsed tissue. It felt like a piece of six-inch steel pipe. No way was that mess going back into this cow. I couldn't believe it. I'd never heard of anything like this. I didn't have a clue. After massaging and manipulating for several minutes, a solution began to form in my mind. I knew that somewhere in all those years in school someone had mentioned a procedure for amputating a rectal prolapse but for the life of me I couldn't even remember where to start.

I was getting desperate. This thing would have to come off but how do you do it? It wasn't like I could just run back to town and look it up. I was thirty miles out and had a full day's work ahead of me. "What the heck," my mother never raised no wimps was my final thought as I grabbed my scalpel and started cutting. It would either work or it wouldn't. Things wouldn't have gotten so grim if the chute I was standing in would have been built differently. It had solid sides and was about seven feet tall with just enough width for a cow to walk down it, kinda like standing in a tunnel with no walls to climb and no room to move around. The significant thing I had forgotten from my lecture notes was the fact that a large artery runs down the top side of the rectum and is looped to the outside when a cow prolapses. This artery is about the size of your thumb as I soon discovered when my scalpel severed it in one easy stroke. Talk about your gusher. The first wave hit me directly between the eyes.

It always amazes me how an artery of this size can squirt blood. It would be like getting hit with a small garden hose under high pressure.

You're immediately soaked. With the walls of the chute I had no where to go. I had to just stand and take it as I desperately tried to snare that artery. Finally after what seemed like hours but couldn't have been more than a minute, I managed to get the slippery little tube shut off with my left hand. That's when I did something really dumb. I decided to just go ahead and cut off the rest of the prolapse. Shoot, it had to come off, didn't it? With my right hand I cut on through and let the hard mass fall to the ground. The great sucking sound I heard was my first warning this was a bad thing to do. The now unattached intestine from inside the cow was sucked back into the abdominal cavity. I now had a large intestine ready to empty itself inside the cow. That's when I did something really dumb. I reached into the cow and started a frantic search for the end of my severed intestine. Luck seemed to have started to come my way. About  twenty inches in I found it, a small miracle considering my inexperience and the confusion of intestines inside a cow.

With steady traction I once again exposed the end to the outside, things were looking up all right. Then my new dilemma struck me, what do I do next. There I stood, the artery in one hand, the intestine in the other hand, my suture material about six feet behind, I seemed to have run out of options. Why hadn't I just repaired the artery immediately? Fortunately I didn't have to make a decision, the up to now patient old cow decided she was sick of this whole mess and proceeded to turn herself inside out as the saying goes. Of course my grip on the slippery tissues was lost instantly as the cow kicked and bucked trying to free her head. Once again the spray of blood was turned loose and like a garden hose it shot out, up and down and back and forth. That cow probably lost a gallon of blood most of it on me. I could feel blood seeping into my underwear. My socks were soaked clear inside my boots as I tried to tie this tenacious squirter off all the while working with a moving target as the cow fought and pulled. Due to the confines of the alley, I couldn't avoid the continuous torrent of red corpuscles.

Eventually I did mange to snare the slippery little hose and took three ties with suture just to make sure, and yes, I did find the intestine one more time inside the cow. What a feeling of relief as I finally turned the old cow loose as patched back together as I was capable of making her. Her chances of survival, about one in a hundred.

Later that afternoon as I shuffled into the office my boss was standing talking to two farmers laughing and joking about some crazy story one had told when all eyes fell on me. The silence suddenly became deafening. Every square inch of me was soaked with blood. After a respectful time was spent paying homage to this wondrous sight, the three started to lose it. Dr. Holt was the first to speak.

"What the devil you been up to now?" he asked after he got his guffaws under control.

The only answer he got and the only one he'll ever get was quite simple.

"I don't wanna talk about it."

Several weeks later the end of the episode occurred one afternoon at the gas station as I was filling up. The owner of the cow came walking out and spotting me, made a bee line over to have a little chat. Boy, was I scared.

"Say, Doc. It must have got a little bloody in the chute the other day, didn't it?" was his greeting.

"Yeah, I'm afraid so." I managed to mutter, "I'm sure sorry about that whole deal. I guess things got a little out of hand."

"A little out of hand, I'd say so. I had no idea a cow could lose that much blood and still live."

My day immediately brightened,

"You mean the old girl is still alive?" I gasped.

"Of course, never missed a beat. Why shouldn't she be? It was just a little prolapse."

How Many Pigs Make A Full Litter?

I never met a pig I liked. Once in a while there might be an old sow that is a little bit tolerable but they are few and far between. The owners of pigs on the other hand are usually pretty good people. They have to be to put up with some of the things pigs say when they are perturbed. Most pigs have a very low discountenance threshold. In other words they'll squeal their fool heads off if they even think you're going to touch them. Get a barn full of pigs and if the smell doesn't get you, the noise is sure to drive you batty. I've heard there are veterinarians who claim to like working on pigs. Believe me, those guys are several strips of bacon short of a pound.

One of the things I do enjoy about our porcine companions is helping a gilt when she has trouble pigging. The best part of pulling pigs is the warmth. No matter the temperature outside, the farrowing house has to be kept warm for the little babies. The atmosphere is always pleasant with the sows grunting at the little guys and the babies squealing at each other as they all look for a milk spigot at the same time. It's really quite restful and relaxing. Many times it takes a couple of hours to get all the little buggers out as they have to work their way down the uterus. There is a lot of sitting around talking between bouts of manipulating another little porker into the world.

Spend a couple of hours with a farmer in the middle of the night pulling pigs while he discusses the world's problems and you start to appreciate the homespun philosophy of people who chose to make a life out of raising hogs. One of my favorite places to pull pigs was out at Harold Phlums. Harold is a storyteller extraordinary, a political pundit, an opinionated S.O.B. and an all around pretty good guy.

This particular night, it was about 11 p.m. as I pulled onto Harold's yard and he started off the evening with a bang.

"Say Doc," he said, "You haven't changed the oil in your pickup the last few days have you?"

Completely baffled, I responded, "No, I sure haven't but what the heck does that have to do with anything?"

"Well if you happened to have a little oil left on your hands, I wouldn't want you reaching in one of my pigs. That will kill a hog every time."

Still completely baffled, I asked, "Now how would you know a thing like that Harold?"

"One time my Dad had a sow that couldn't get her pigs. He worked on her for two days till he finally got the last pig out. Three days later she died, no reason, just died. We finally figured out it had to be that he'd changed oil in the tractor the day before he started and had some left on his hands. That oil killed her dead."

Harold gave me a look of complete incredulousness when I replied, "Don't suppose you ever considered it might be his lack of skill that had anything to do with it, did you?"

The silence hung over the farrowing house like a wet blanket for awhile as I prepared my instruments and gently felt inside my recumbent patient. Harold, with his natural exuberance couldn't stay pensive for long, even though I had greatly insulted the memory of his dear old dad.

"Hey Doc." he said, "Bet you don't know how to tell for sure when a sow doesn't have any more pigs left in her."

"No," I replied, "That's something we could make a million dollars on. There's just no way to know for sure when a pig is done except to open her up and look. If you have a sure fire method, we'll patent it."

"Well, my dad taught me so you probably don't even want to hear about it. He wasn't an educated vet like you."

"No kidding," was my rather sarcastic remark. "I'll bet I'm going to hear about it, though, before the night's over."

Everything was quiet for awhile as I quickly extracted two little pigs from the sow, making a total of six counting the four that had come before I arrived. Now it was time to wait awhile until some more pigs came down the chute.

Harold started out slow this time, "Hey, Doc. Bet you don't know why a pig never chews its cud like a cow does."

"That's an easy one, Harold. A pig doesn't have a rumen, so can't have a cud. It takes a rumen to have a cud."

"Nope, want to give it another try?"

"Maybe it's because they eat too much used oil from tractors and cars – that makes the stomach contents too slippery to be regurgitated."

"Nope, but you're getting closer. Give up?"

"I know. It's because they eat a lot of fruits and vegetables so they don't have to rechew the soggy mess inside. That's got to be right."

"Nope, I'm surprised they didn't teach you these things in college. You know I almost went to college but my Dad wouldn't let me. He was scared I'd dumb up."

"Now you have to tell me, Harold. What in the world is dumb up? Is that kinda like a lack of horse sense?"

"Yep, to dumb up is to waste so much time in school you never learn why a pig doesn't have a cud or how to tell if any pigs are left inside."

"Really?" It took a lot of patience to have a conversation with Harold.

"Hey, Doc. Bet you don't know why some sheep have black lambs do you?"

"I'll bet a hundred dollars it doesn't have anything to do with genetics and DNA, does it?"

"Nope, it sure doesn't. Give up?"

"You know what I think? I think you should write a textbook for all the veterinary students to use. Then they would come out of school knowing all this stuff."

Harold was beaming, sarcasm was not his forte.

"OK, guess I'll just have to give you a lesson in barnyard common sense. Pigs don't chew a cud 'cause they don't have back grinders like a cow. Their teeth are not flat like a cow's teeth. And black lambs come from the ewe getting scared by a black dog when she was pregnant. My daddy would shoot any black dog that came around during the fall. Those black lambs cost money you know."

"Shooting dogs seems a little extreme. Did it always work?"

"Nope, sometimes those black dogs would sneak around during the night and you'd get a black lamb no matter how careful you was."

Things were quiet in the farrowing house as I digested all this wisdom, but Harold couldn't be quiet for long.

"Think there are any left, Doc?

"Yeah, probably. We'll just have to wait awhile and see if we get anymore action," I answered as I gave my patient a shot of oxytocin to stimulate her uterus to contract a little quicker.

The delivery slowly progressed as the little pigs continued to show up one about every fifteen minutes or so and I gently extracted them from the now swollen vagina.

Our conversation followed the full gamut of topics we had in common, the price of corn, the price of cattle, the price of wheat, the price of hogs, the inflated price of veterinary services, all the local gossip, all the national politicians until finally we both knew it had to be getting close to the end. We now had twelve pigs nuzzling the sow each looking for its fair share of milk.

"I'll tell you what, Harold. I think she's done, but I sure hate to leave too quickly and have to come back after one more of the little buggers."

"She's not done, Doc. Believe me, I can tell."

"I don't know. She's grunting like a sow that's done, and she's passed a lot of afterbirth – two pretty good signs she might be empty."

"I'll bet you double or nothing on your bill that she's not done yet." This with a twinkle in his eye. He was, as always, very sure of himself and too smug for his own good.

At this point I broke one of my cardinal rules: never bet with a farmer. There are two reasons for this rule: First, I just about always end up losing money, and second, when I don't lose money, I just about always end up with a farmer upset with me when he has to pay up.

"OK, the bets on but I'm so sure of myself on this one I'm going to pack up my stuff and go get some sleep. Tell me though how come you're so sure there's a pig left inside?"

"Just take a real close look, Doc. Do you see anything different about what this pig is doing than what a pig that is done farrowing does? Take a close look and think about it."

After watching the sow for a moment, I had to confess, she just looked like any other sow to me.

"I'm sorry but I can't see anything different."

"I'll give you a hint, Doc. Which way does a sow twirl her tail when she's pregnant?"

"What are you talking about. There are no rules to which way a pig twirls its tail. That's the craziest thing I ever heard of."

"All I know is what my daddy told me. He wasn't a college-educated man, of course, but he knew a few things. I've watched over the years and it always works. She'll twirl clockwise when she's pregnant and counter when she's not. Never fails."

"Harold, Harold, Harold, you can come up with the weirdest ideas some times. I feel guilty taking your money. Maybe we better just call the bet off, OK?"

"A bet's a bet where I come from. You getting cold feet, Doc.?"

"Even if by some miracle it was true, how could that tail know immediately when the last pig was out and she was no longer pregnant? I'm afraid your whole idea just doesn't make a lot of sense."

With this parting shot I opened the door and started out to my truck with all my gear, shaking my head as I went.

As I was loading my truck, Harold called from the door of the hog house, "Hey Doc, she's acting a little funny. Maybe you better take a last look before you go."

You guessed it, just as I walked up to the farrowing crate that old sow gave a heave and out popped another little pig, big as life.

Harold's parting words still grate on me whenever I remember that night.

"It's a shame you have to come out on a cold night and end up not even getting paid for it, isn't it, Doc?"

Little Old Ladies

Little old ladies and ornery cats are not a good mix. They both expect too much out of the world and seem to lack common sense when it comes to getting shots, exams and various other functions of their veterinarians. Martha was one of my little old ladies that just couldn't seem to grasp the simple truth, that truth being that some

cats just don't make good pets. Martha was a widow and her pets had become her whole life. She was somewhere around 75 years old and had the audacity of old age when it came to telling others how to run their lives and businesses.

"Twinky just hasn't been himself lately, and his breath has gotten so bad I hate to even kiss him anymore." This was the first clue Martha gave me as she set the carrier on my exam table and gently extracted a large black tom cat whom I had never met before. Red flags and alarms went off so loud in my head it sounded like the fire department had arrived as Twinky gave me a look of complete hatred followed by a low deep snarl.

"Oh Twinky, you're such a tease. Don't worry, Doctor. He is just a big pussy cat. He wouldn't hurt a fly." This was her reaction to his hissing and growling as I gently tried to stroke his back and sides. After a number of tries, I managed to get a look at several large yellow teeth covered with tartar so thick the teeth themselves couldn't be seen.

"I'm afraid those teeth are in rather bad shape, Martha. We'll have to get them cleaned right away or he may end up losing some. There may be a few beyond help already. Where did you get this cat anyway?"

"Oh, he wandered into the yard one day and I just fell in love with him. He's such a dear."

"It would be a good idea to give him his shots while we're at it too, never know about a stray cat."

Just as I uttered these words Twinky decided he was sick and tired of my attentions and told me so by quickly taking a rather "gentle" swipe over my left thumb. Blood instantly oozed out of four identical lines.

Even though she was watching my every move, Martha's reaction was predictable: "Twinky, you bad boy. You scratched the Doctor, you must be a good little kitty or the doctor won't let you come back."

"He acts like he could get a little feisty," I muttered, as I used a paper towel to stop the blood from seeping out.

"You just have to be gentle with him. He's had a hard life. You can be gentle, can't you?" she said with a hint of sarcasm.

"Maybe you can get him back into his cage. We'll just store him in there until we can get at him," I answered feebly.

Later that afternoon, the fun began. Somehow I figured we could get along if it was just the two of us, Twinky and I. What a mistake! But heck, you have to have a little excitement around the clinic once in a while. As I reached into the pet carrier with gloved hand to extract my now quiet patient for his shot of anesthesia, Twinky decided this time for sure he didn't like anything about this whole idea. Quick as a flash, with all four paws unsheathed, and several dozen yellow teeth mashing, he extracted himself from the cage with no help from me. Out of the cage and up the wall, did you ever see a frightened cat climb a wall? Good old Twinky, up the wall and bounce off the corner – then around the room a couple of times and back up the wall clear to the ceiling, bounce off the corner and back down, all the time yowling like someone was yanking his tail out by the roots. I was starting to get the impression he wasn't very enamored with my gentle manner. After several trips around the ceiling of the exam room, he managed to find a hole just big enough to slip into behind the refrigerator. By craning my neck, I could just see him backed into the hole with two big yellow eyes shining, mad at the whole world, especially me. I needed reinforcements.

A few minutes later my hired man Keith and I gently entered the exam room. I had my hog snare at the ready; Twinky might have won a couple of battles but I would win the war.

"You poke him out and I'll snare the bugger as he goes by." I had an easy solution to the dilemma.

"Sure, Doc. Here he comes!" Keith quickly responded.

It didn't work. He came out just a little too fast for me. Up the wall around the room howling at the top of his voice, Twinky was really getting worked up now. Disaster! My partner, Dr. Holt, who must have thought we were killing that poor cat, opened the door to see what was going on. Good old Twinky climbed him just like he was a ladder, catapulted from on top his head all the way across the room to the hanging plant above the water cooler and for several seconds hung on the plant surveying the reception area for the best escape from his tormentors. Disaster! One of our unfavorite drug salesmen opened the outside door to come in.

"CLOSE THE DOOR!!" came from three mouths simultaneously.

"Grab that cat!" I hollered as Twinky quickly took advantage of the open daylight and headed for parts unknown. The salesman just wasn't lucky. He made a grab as Twinky went by and managed to grasp the last thing out the door, which, of course, was Twinky's big black tail. Believe me, you never grab a mad cat by the tail. It just isn't a very good idea. Quick as a cat! Twinky decided to punish the impudence of some idiot that would dare to touch his precious anatomy. Ripping and slashing, he climbed up that poor guy so fast he must have thought he'd grabbed a mountain lion. Funny what four whipping claws can do to a twenty-dollar silk tie, not to mention the damage they can do to a suit coat, as they make their way up to the

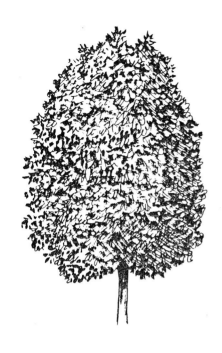

top. The poor salesman decided he'd better let go just as Twinky reached his shoulder. Free at last, Twinky made good his escape and like a streak, he was up the large maple tree that stands in front of the clinic.

Funny how things like this always attract a crowd. Within minutes it seemed like everyone in town was under the maple tree giving advice and comments.

"What the heck were you doing to that poor cat?"

"You better call the fire department."

"Poke him with a stick."

"Throw some rocks at him."

"Set some food at the base of the tree, He'll come down."

"Were you trying to neuter him, Doc? No wonder he's mad. I'd be mad too."

It's a good thing I have a resourceful hired man. Good old Keith always has an idea. Within a few minutes here he came with a thirty-foot lariat rope in hand and a grin on his face. Keith always loves to show off in front of a crowd.

"You folks better stand back a little," Keith commented as he took charge of crowd control. "This could get a little nasty."

With that he quickly scrambled up the tree with lariat in hand while my partner and I stood with hog holder and cage, acting like we knew what we were doing.

Within seconds both Keith and Twinky were lost in the leaves, out of sight somewhere high up where the branches get small and it's a long way to the ground.

We knew they were both doing their jobs by several exclamations from on high, "I'll get you now you @#%@½&**@%½½." This from Keith, followed by, "Aroooooooooooooooooooo, hiss, spit, hiss, Arooooooooo."

"#@½@½½$&*&%@@#½½/," followed by breaking branches and falling leaves.

The crowd on the ground had grown to a dozen by now and the advice kept coming. This was better than the last carnival to come to town.

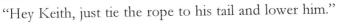

"Put some salt on his tail, Keith."

"Find a female cat and tempt him down."

"Do you guys do this sort of thing all the time?"

"What are you trying to do to that poor animal?"

"Hey Keith, just tie the rope to his tail and lower him."

All the time the conversation from the top of the tree continued, "I'll get you, you @@$%½½½**##."

"Hiss, snarl, Arooooooooooooo."

The whole tree episode ended rather abruptly, much to the audience's disappointment. Suddenly with much cracking of branches, swearing, hissing, yowling and commotion, down came Keith and Twinky intertwined and both so busy with each other's company they never noticed the impending ground coming at them. At the last second, seemingly in unison, they both realized their predicament and grabbed the lowest branch which was about eight feet off the ground. There they hung by one hand or paw looking each other in the eye and continuing their conversation.

Dr. Holt, who never seems to lose his cool, quickly stepped up with the cage, opened the door, and gently forced Twinky inside. It looked like those two had planned the whole thing all along. The audience and I stood in awed silence.

"Good work, Keith," Dr. Holt commented as he headed back into the clinic with Twinky still growling and hissing between the bars.

The next morning Martha was right on time. How could she stand another day without her little darling.

"Did he give you any trouble Doctor?" she inquired as she peered into the cage at the rather contrite Twinky.

"No, of course not," I answered through gritted teeth.

"It's just like I told you. You have to be gentle with these animals and they'll be gentle with you."

Manure Spreaders Have A Lot Of Uses

Sometimes you think it couldn't get any weirder out there and then along comes a group like the Thompson brothers. These guys had a monopoly on doing things their own way, which was usually a lot different from the way the rest of the world functioned.

I never did get their names straight and to this day I couldn't tell them apart. I think the oldest one was named George. He was the spokesperson for the bunch, or maybe the middle one did the talking. Who could tell?

The most noticeable characteristic which immediately caught your eye was their absolute, long standing, ground-in dirt and filth. In the years I did some occasional work for them I never saw a sign of cleaned clothes, shaved faces, combed hair, or any other personal hygiene. Their clothes would be so dirty you could no longer tell the color of the shirt that poked out between the blue bibs on their coveralls. All three always wore blue coveralls, blue work shirts (I suspect), old straw hats, lace up work shoes with no socks, and the ugliest scraggliest beards imaginable. All three chewed snooze and let it dribble down their chins through their beards and drop somewhere on the blue bib. This trio would top the scale at about 360 pounds if they all jumped on together, not very big but what they lacked in size they made up for by being lazy. I kind of liked the Thompson brothers. You got what you paid for – no guile with this crew.

In the winter time the straw hats would be replaced by red plaid winter caps, and they would all put on insulated blue jean jackets. Add to this a pair of five buckle overshoes and their entire wardrobe was accounted for.

The first time I saw the brothers I was at the local sale barn inspecting cattle when they arrived with the skinniest old cow you can imagine. The cow itself wasn't as remarkable as the method they had of conveying her. George was driving their Model B John Deere tractor hooked to an old fashioned manure spreader. In the manure spreader were the other two Thompsons sitting on either side, with the old cow riding comfortably between them. She was tied to the front of the spreader with a short strand of rope but nothing else was keeping her in this strange wagon.

If you're not familiar with the old paddle type manure spreaders, they are two wheeled trailers that hook to a tractor and have big paddles on the back which are hooked by a chain to the wheels. When engaged, the paddles go around and spread the manure across the field. On the floor of this useful apparatus is a conveyer belt made of steel bars that also engages with the paddles and makes the manure move back to the paddles until the entire load is spread. All in all a very useful way to organically fertilize your fields. The sides on these wagons are only about two feet high so they only came up to the cow's belly line, leaving most of the beast high in the air as if riding in a parade.

This particular day as George and the boys pulled up to the sale barn, they soon collected an audience of interested livestock pundits, comedians, authorities on all things, and general hang-arounders who are always present at the sale barn. They soon started trying to outdo themselves to get a laugh.

"You boys have a commercial license to haul livestock?"

"Why didn't you bring a whole load while you were coming?"

"Do you guys have a patent on that livestock hauler you invented?"

"Put her in gear, George, and unload the old rip. We can sell her as hamburger."

With this last statement the crowd suddenly became rather quiet as they all had the same thought. How were the boys going to unload that old cow? And another thought, how in the world did they get her loaded to begin with? You can't just ask a skinny old cow to kindly step into a manure spreader and then hop out again when you have her at the auction.

What no one had taken into consideration was the ability of people that were used to living in a world of broken machinery, baling wire repairs, and a lack of money so acute you had to learn to make do with whatever you could. Even if it meant hauling your cattle to market in the manure spreader. The Thompsons were "can do" guys.

Without a word to any of the wisecrackers, George pulled the old poppin' Johnny up beside the unloading chute, pulled the pin to unhook his strange wagon, then wheeled the tractor around until it faced the spreader which had fallen on its tongue. The other two brothers quickly jumped out, untied the cow and retied the rope to the front of the John Deere. With the rope now around the cow's neck and tied to the tractor they grabbed a couple of bridge planks from inside the spreader and balanced them over the front of the spreader facing the tractor. They were now ready to start unloading. With both brothers behind the cow, George started to slowly back up and low and behold, the old cow slid up the planks on her belly. Her legs caught for a second but the boys quickly lifted them over the front of the spreader so the cow now hung half in and half out, still going mostly uphill. As the trusty Model B continued to apply pressure, the old cow eased forward until her weight shifted to the outside and down came the planks, out came the cow catching herself with all four feet now on the ground. With that they led the cow into the salebarn, hooked back up to the spreader and headed downtown to do some shopping. The salebarn crowd was very quiet for a long time until one of them asked the obvious, "That was simple to figure out but how do you suppose they loaded the old girl?"

The Thompson boys weren't through: They had some money in their pockets, time on their hands, and a mighty thirst. This was probably their first trip to town in weeks. It gets mighty cold riding in the back of a manure spreader for fifteen miles during a Dakota winter. I learned later this strange contraption was their only means of transportation. They had no cars nor pickups. Usually about once a month you would see them either coming or going, one guy on the Model B and the other two in the spreader. If they happened to be going home, the whole crew would be higher than a kite waving beer cans and singing at the top of their lungs. Can you get picked up for driving under the influence if you're driving a John Deere?

No one I ever talked to had been inside the Thompson brother's ramshackle old house, no one until that eventful day when both Keith and I were invited in for lunch.

It all started with a call from one of their neighbors one warm spring day in April. It seemed as if the brothers had a problem with a cow that had just calved.

"George needs to talk to you, Doc. He has a problem," was my first warning on the phone.

"Her insides are out and flopping all over the place," was George's breathless announcement. "We need some help, Doc."

They needed some help all right! What an understatement! The poor old cow was down with about ten gallons of uterus out behind her. Her eyes were sunk and hidden so far back you needed a flashlight to see if anyone was still in there. Keith and I had been here before. Without wasting a minute we had an I.V. going and were busily working on the uterus trying to get the entire mess back inside the cow. Many times on a bad uterine prolapse, you can essentially give the cow a blood transfusion, so to speak, if you can get the uterus back and make all the blood in it once again available to the cow. Speed is of the essence. They can die quickly.

We knew we were in trouble even without George's wry comment as we struggled, "I think you're working on a dead cow, Doc."

Sure enough, she was dead all right.

I just hate that feeling. One minute you're full of hope. The adrenaline is pumping, and you just know you can win this one. The next minute it's all over. You lost. The first few minutes are especially hard.

You have to make small talk and try to explain how you did every-thing you could but she was just too far gone, etc. etc. etc.

George and his brothers felt worse about the way I was feeling than they did about losing the cow. I'm sure it was this weakness that prompted him to ask, "Let's go have some coffee, Doc. You'll feel better with a little hot coffee."

Things were looking up. Could this house be as bad as we all imagined? Were there re-ally rats on the countertops? Was the rumor true that chick-ens roosted on the Cheerios box? Did the dog have his own place at the table? Did pigeons really fly through the dining

room and roost above the china cabinet? Was it true the goats were used as bed warmers? Finally all the questions would be answered and Keith and I would be the experts! The next time one of the coffee shop set made a comment on the Thompsons, I could see myself calmly clearing my throat and becoming an instant celebrity with the simple statement, "I've been inside boys. Let me tell you some stories."

It wasn't as bad as everyone thought. It was worse, a lot worse. As we stepped into the front porch, it was apparent the old house didn't have many years left in it. One had to step down onto a dirt floor as the wooden floor of the porch had long ago disappeared, and then step up onto a cement block which worked as a step into the kitchen. After we entered the kitchen, things really got grim. Can you believe baby pigs under the kitchen table? This place made Ma and Pa Kettle look like the Vanderbilts.

Without going into detail let me say it wasn't the type of setting where one would expect a chocolate cake to stimulate the appetite. With a grimy old stained cup in hand, I slowly sipped a lukewarm brew that tasted a lot like coffee. It had to be sterile was my reasoning. It was boiled wasn't it? Looking across the table I saw a sight that gladdened my heart and made me feel warm all over – I saw the perfect chance to nail old Keith. I mean nail him good. Keith, being Keith had accepted a piece of chocolate cake from an old pan one of the boys had obviously spent several long arduous minutes baking. On top of the cake, probably to make it appear more visually appetizing, our cook had sprinkled some powdered sugar, which gave me my great idea. I quickly looked away, not wanting to make him suspicious. The wrong look could spoil everything.

Later, with Keith driving, we were headed back to town comparing notes on the whole experience when I started my scheme to humble old Keith once and for all.

"That was quite an experience all right," was my opening salvo, "I was sure surprised at what you did though."

"What do you mean, what did I do?"

"Oh nothing, it just seemed a little out of character, I guess."

"What's that supposed to mean?"

"Oh just forget it, I shouldn't have said anything, it's not important."

With that I let a few miles go by as he continued to stew.

"Come on, Doc. What are you talking about? You can't just leave me high and dry."

"Just leave it be, Keith. Believe me, you don't want to know."

This really got him going. He would die to know what I was talking about. It's a great feeling when a well thought out plan starts to work. You see, I knew Keith had a rather weak stomach when his imagination was properly stimulated, which was my next step.

"I was just a little surprised when you ate that cake was all," I said in my most sympathetic voice.

Suddenly a very meek Keith, something seldom if ever seen before, was asking, "Please Doc, you have to tell me. What was wrong with the cake?"

"Oh it probably won't hurt you any. The old human stomach is pretty resilient."

"Holy cow, man, what the devil was wrong with the cake?"

"Keith, you idiot, didn't you see that white growth on top. What the heck do you think it was?"

"Uh, I don't know, I guess I didn't think much about it."

It was time for the coup, "Did you ever hear of mold, Keith? Man, I could have gotten enough penicillin off that cake to treat a horse."

Did you ever see a pick-up doing sixty miles an hour on a gravel road stop in fifty feet? It's a little scary but it was worth it. Life was good! What a wonderful day!

Soon I would be stopping for coffee in town and casually mentioning as I sit down, "Yep, I had lunch out at the Thompson's today. You think the cow in the manure spreader is strange. You should see what they have in the kitchen sink."

Farm Dogs Are Family Too

Farm dogs are pretty good people most of the time. Unlike many other members of the farmer's menagerie, the dog can often get away with things that do not directly contribute to the financial well-being of the endeavor. This pandering only goes so far though, and no matter how good a friend he's been, he'd better take care of himself if misfortune should strike. Most farmers just cannot justify spending good money on a member that doesn't contribute. Sometimes it seems cruel to see a dog neglected as far as medical attention but the same rules apply to the cattle and sheep: produce or else. I feel like a winner if I can get the average farmer to at least vaccinate the dog for rabies – for distemper and other diseases, not a chance.

The only domestic animals lower on the scale than dogs are the barn cats. The cats are there for one reason, to keep the mice population under control. The conventional wisdom is that a hungry cat will catch more mice than a well-fed cat, so they maybe get a little milk if some is left after the bucket calf gets his feeding, but cat food is usually unheard of.

This whole attitude makes for some interesting situations: farm dogs and cats are forever tangling with mowers, cars, pickups, tractors, power take off shafts, horses, cows, coyote traps, and various other mechanical and non-mechanical dangers. The farmers comment is usually about the same, "He's been a pretty good dog, Doc. See what you can do but we sure don't want to get too spendy. We can always get a new pup if we have to."

This when you're looking at a broken femur or perhaps a half-dozen mower cuts that will take two hours to suture.

One thing you learn working under these circumstances: animals are a lot tougher than we give them credit for. Their healing abilities are extraordinary compared to a human with a similar injury. I have seen cats with broken bones sticking through the skin undergo complete recovery with no human interference.

Before we get too hard on farmers, we want to realize that most barn cats are for all practical purposes feral animals. Most of them cannot be caught and petted and are a far cry from the pampered tabbies that live in suburbia.

One of my favorite friends on the farm was a funny old black dog named Ace. Ace was just a mutt with a little bit of every breed under the sun poking out from his DNA. His legs were short and fat suggesting perhaps a touch of basset; his tail was long and bushy suggesting a touch of collie; his ears were long and hung down suggesting a touch of spaniel; his body was long and curved suggesting a touch of dachshund; and his mouth was black suggesting a touch of chow. Ace was quite a study in genetic engineering. The most endearing trait that Ace always showed was his smile. He could grin from ear to ear and wiggle his entire misproportioned body a hundred wiggles a second if he was glad to see you, and he was always glad to see you. Ace in his exuberance had a knack for getting in trouble. That's were I usually entered his life.

My first encounter with this walking accident occurred one hot summer day when I was sitting around the office hoping nothing would happen that required any effort. The entire Johnson family which consisted of Sam, his wife Karen and their five kids ranging in age from about two years to about ten came driving up to the clinic where I sat sunning myself. All the kids started shouting before the car had even stopped.

"We have a hurt puppy. Can you help us?"
"We found him out on the road."
"Someone must have left him."
"Will he be OK.?"

The questions rolled out so fast I had to wave my arms to get a comment in.

"Come on in and we'll have a look at this little bugger."

As I gently began my exam, Sam filled in the details.

"We found him out on the highway, must have been hit by a car, looks like his leg is broke to me. I'd like to fix him up if it isn't too spendy, Doc. Kids could use a pup."

The strange looking little black dog with the floppy ears was a sad sight, scared to death with dust and grease smeared all over. It was hard to believe a car could hit such a tiny little thing and not completely smash it. As I ended my examination, it was easy to tell we had at least one major problem.

"Looks like his leg is broke all right. We'll need some X-rays to tell for sure what all is wrong though."

It didn't take Karen long to pick up on the significance of this statement. She didn't mince around.

"What will that cost?"

"Yeah," said Sam, "We wouldn't want to spend that kind of money. Couldn't you just fix him up a little without all the fuss?"

Karen, always the realist piped in again, "Maybe we should have just left him. I knew this would get out of hand. Can't you just put him to sleep? What would that run?"

I could tell there hadn't been a lot of bonding between the parents and their new puppy yet. What can you say?

"Maybe we could just put a splint on the leg and see what happens. There doesn't seem to be anything else too major going on. Who knows? These little pups heal really fast most the time."

Karen liked the sound of this, "Yeah that sounds like a good idea. The kids can take care of him. He should be OK."

As I finished wrapping the molded splint with Vet Wrap, the leg seemed to fit back together rather well and my hopes began to rise.

"It looks pretty good to me. Let's just let him wear this thing for a couple of weeks and see what happens. With a little luck we should be OK."

The leg healed without a blemish and straight as possible on a pup with crooked legs to begin with. Ace was a lucky little dog all right or so we all thought until the next time he screwed up and got into trouble. The next time just happened to be two weeks after we had removed the first splint.

This time it was just Sam that showed up with the now twelve-week old Ace and it didn't look good. Ace had somehow managed to get his nose into a bag of mouse poison and had gotten an obvious overdose of warfarin – a potent anticoagulant. Warfarin works by destroying the blood's ability to clot so the animal will slowly bleed to death usually inside but sometimes out the nose or intestines. The poor little thing looked a fright with a slow-drip nosebleed, labored breathing, and just plain feeling like crap. I knew it would be a tough one. Sam soon told me the problem.

"He ate some rat poison, Doc. I was hopin' you could do somethin'. The kids really like the little guy. We can't get too spendy though. A new pup is pretty cheap."

I gave him my best shot.

"It will take a few days of Vitamin K therapy to have any chance at all. I'm afraid it doesn't look good, Sam. I better keep him here until we are over the hump. We might even need some blood to get him going again."

"I'd rather you just gave him some shots and we'll take our chances. Maybe you could send some pills with me and the kids can take care of him. He'll be OK."

"Sam!" I exclaimed, "You have to realize how sick he is. Why if this was a human baby, he would be in intensive care and they would spend thousands of dollars on him. You can't expect miracles if you don't give him a fighting chance."

Once again he got right to the heart of the problem, "How much would all that cost, Doc?"

I sent Ace home with a week's supply of Vitamin K tablets. His chances looked like one in a million to me.

Several months went by and I never heard another word about my little waif of a patient until one cold winter night as I sat quietly minding my own business watching "Seinfeld." The phone rang with that ear shattering roar it can only make on a cold winter night. Karen was on the other end.

"Doc, we had an accident. Can we come right in?"

"Yes, of course, but what seems to be the problem?"

"It's Ace. Sam picked him up in some hay with the grapple fork and it looks really bad. We just have to save him. The kids have gotten too attached. He's just like one of the family to them. Can we come right in?"

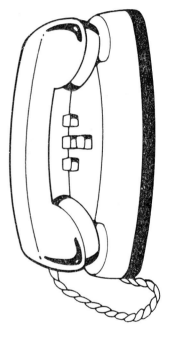

"I'll meet you at the clinic in fifteen minutes or so. Is he bleeding a lot?"

"No, but there is a great big hole in his side. It really looks bad."

Once again I knew this was going to be a tough one. Ace had a hole in his flank as big as my fist with another hole on the opposite side about the size of a silver dollar. Had the grapple fork tine gone clear through him? I just couldn't see how this could be possible as I began my exam, but did not see any other possibilities.

Let me explain a grapple fork: the tines are long, curved, pointed pieces of steel which go up and down. A hydraulic cylinder makes them move. It is used to grapple, as the name implies, a large bale or pile of hay with the loader while keeping the hay from falling off. Most loaders used to feed cattle will have three tines on the front end.

In this case Sam was loading hay from a stack not knowing that Ace was sleeping in the hay pile. As the fork came down, one of the tines impaled the little guy. As bad as it sounds, Ace wasn't too upset by the whole thing. His tail was still wagging a mile a minute and he grinned at me as if this was the greatest thing in the world. After all, it isn't every night one gets to go to town and get so much attention.

I opened with my usual statement, "It looks pretty bad, you guys. We'll have to get him anesthetized and do some probing in this hole to see how bad it really is."

It was Karen's turn, "I just hope it doesn't get too spendy, Doc. I know he's a good little dog but a new pup is sure easy to come by."

Was there a chink in the armor? She hadn't said an absolute no.

Sam spoke up, "You do what you can, Doc. But what will it cost?"

A definite chink. I had my answer ready, "I'll do what I can and it won't be over $100. I promise."

One of my rules with myself is that when I give an estimate, I live with it no matter what. Sometimes I end up doing some work for nothing but in the long run it makes for mighty good feelings when the job is done.

Sam and Karen exchanged glances like married couples do when making a decision.

"OK," said Sam, "we can live with that. Just do what you can."

Ace and I got lucky. The tine had punctured the skin in the flank area leaving the big hole, but as luck would have it, it had slid under the skin all the way around the abdominal cavity to the other side where it had come out again. By some miracle the cavity itself was not injured. My job was quite easy. All I had to do was close the two holes in the skin and load him up with antibiotics. This time my estimate was a good one. I charged them $65 and they were happy as

61

punch. Ace went home the next day still grinning, unruffled as always and still not realizing what all the fuss was about. He made an uneventful recovery.

It was several years before I saw Ace as a patient again. He would always be underfoot when we were working cattle or vaccinating pigs, the ever present grin in place and the perpetual flag waving from between our legs or out around the pens. He seemed to live a mighty good life but you could tell he was always on the edge. The next big crisis came on Christmas Day when Ace was four years old.

It was Karen on the phone in tears, "It's Ace. He's really done it this time. Can we bring him in right away?"

"Yes of course, what seems to be the matter?"

"He got under the wheel on the big tractor. It looks really bad."

"I'll meet you at the clinic in fifteen minutes. Maybe it isn't as tough as it looks."

Ace wasn't grinning and his tail was still. The X-ray looked like every bone from the ribs on back were broken or out of place. A big tractor tire is an awesome thing.

I was as gentle as I could be, "I'm sorry guys. This is beyond anything I can handle. Maybe if we could get him to the University of Minnesota Veterinary School, he would have a chance but that would cost a ton, I'm afraid."

Karen was the first to speak, "That would really get spendy, I'm sure."

Sam jumped in, "How much do you think Doc?"

Could these be the same people I'd been talking to for four years?

"I don't know but I could call in the morning and see what they think. I'm sure it could get up around a thousand dollars, maybe more."

Sam's eyes got as big as saucers, "I don't know. The kids sure do like this dog though."

Karen looked like she could keel over, "That's more than a good cow is worth."

I could see there might be a chance but I wasn't going to push anything. "Why don't you guys just go on home and think the whole thing over. I'll stabilize him as good as I can for tonight and you can decide in the morning. Nothing much can be done on Christmas Day anyway."

It was a sad little family that left my office. I often wonder why so many times bad things have to happen on Christmas Day. I did what I could for my patient. He didn't seem to be in danger of dying so it was mostly just a matter of keeping him warm and hydrated to stop the shock.

About an hour later there was a knock on my door and who should be there but Sam. I knew what he wanted — they had decided on euthanasia. Boy, was I surprised.

"Doc." He started out, "I know Karen won't approve but I'm gonna go ahead and take Ace to Minneapolis in the mornin'. I've got a little corn left we can sell. That should cover the cost. I just wanted you to

know so you could do all you can gettin' him ready."

"Sam, I think that's wonderful and you just wait. Karen will come around."

Much to my surprise the big tough farmer suddenly choked up and tears slowly slipped down his cheek.

"You know, Doc," He finally managed to get out, "the kids really love that little dog."

"I know, Sam. I understand."

After Sam had left, it was at least five minutes before the phone rang. I barely had my composure back. It was Karen.

"Doc," She started out, "I know Sam won't approve but I'm going to take Ace to Minneapolis in the morning. I've got some money saved up that should cover the cost. I just wanted you to know so you could do all you can getting him ready."

"Karen, I think that's wonderful and you just wait, Sam will come around."

She broke into tears. "I don't know, Doc. But the kids really love that little dog."

"Karen," I said with certainty, "I guarantee Sam will think this is a great idea."

Ace made an uneventful recovery and the bill was only $1500.

Cows Can Talk Too, You Know

Did you ever watch a cat watch a blank space? He sees something we don't see and other cats will often pick up on it. My three cats will be sitting around doing cat things like sleeping when all of sudden I might notice one cat completely immersed in a happening in the corner of the room or on the empty chair. In a few minutes all three cats will be awake and looking at the strange goings on. When it's over, they will all three relax and go back to sleep. It drives me crazy. They are seeing something I can't see and telling each other about it. I can be made to feel very inferior by my feline buddies at such times. I wish they would or could share it with me and you know I'm almost certain they are trying their best to do just that if I would somehow learn to pay attention. Cattle have the same kind of internal communication but I think it is small potatoes compared to cats. I first really started paying attention to this ability in cows when I met the triplets, Molly, Helen, and Bertha.

It was the worst possible time for the phone to ring, 10 p.m. I was absolutely pooped from being out too much at night and working too hard during the day. Bedtime was here and I felt I darn well deserved a good night's rest. I guess we all have our day-dreams.

It was Curt Anderson on the other end of the line with the good news.

"I've got an old cow that's been at it since six, Doc, and I just can't seem to figure it out. She seems to have six legs comin' and no head."

"Yeah, they can really be a bugger to figure out, did you try to pull at all on the little snot?"

I wanted to get an idea how tough this would likely be so I could get myself mentally prepared on the road.

"No, I figured I better leave it alone till you got here. I wouldn't want to mess things up."

Good news, sounded like an easy one, probably twins, just figure out which legs went with which calf and pull the little guys out. My favorite kind of obstetrical case.

Curt was one of my best ranchers. He was very capable but knew his limitations and saw to it things got done around the place. His calving area was always bedded with clean straw and well lit, no laying in the mud with a flashlight on this place. When he called, you knew it would be a hard one but he always appreciated your work and would tell you so. Even well-paid vets need a pat on the back once in a while.

As I groped my way around the several legs inside the old cow, I

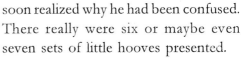

soon realized why he had been confused. There really were six or maybe even seven sets of little hooves presented.

Curt soon continued his commentary, "Did you ever feel such a tangled up mess in your life? There must be four or five of the little buggers in there. I sure couldn't make heads or tails out of it. How do you figure something like that out anyway?"

As I continued my exploration inside the cow, I explained to him how you handle a confused group of limbs all trying to find the outside at the same time.

"The first thing you do is find a back leg by feeling down one until you come to a hock. That way you don't have to worry about the head and where it is. Next you hook on to that leg with a rope or chain and give a little traction to get it as far out as possible. Then the hard part comes; reaching down the leg and finding the pelvis, feeling around the pelvis until you find the leg coming out the other side, come out to the hoof, hook on and pull the calf, easy as pie sometimes."

No sooner said than done as I slipped a wet unhappy camper out into the world, followed a few minutes later with another little beggar the mirror image of the first, and just as upset about leaving her warm waterbed in the middle of the night. Sure enough as I reached back inside there were still two sets of little hooves presenting themselves.

"Your lucky day, Curt, there must be at least three of the little critters, maybe four or five who knows?"

As I slipped out the third calf, he voiced his disappointment with the multiple birth.

"I was just hoping for one good heifer from this old girl. She's my best cow and I'd sure like a heifer or two from her to keep as a replacement before she gets too old."

As I checked the sex of the little group once again, I told him of his luck.

"All three seem to be heifers, Curt, so you can keep the whole bunch for replacements if you want to. This is your lucky day."

He felt a lot better after I explained to him the problems of keeping twin calves for breeding applies only to a heifer born twin to a bull calf. The male hormones produced by the male calf will seep through the placenta of the female and usually make her sterile. Heifers born together are no problem.

"We'll have to see what happens, but it would sure be great to keep all three of them for cows someday," was his now cheerful outlook as we watched the three little calves get their first good cleaning by mom.

The best time to be a veterinarian was right now, a successful birth, the smell of warm fresh straw in a warm barn and a gentle old cow licking her new found friend while talking to the little guy or in this case little girls.

I spent a lot of time at Curt's ranch that spring. It was a cold wet April and the calf scours, pneumonia, and other baby calf problems were severe. It was about three weeks after our late night sojourn that Curt first mentioned the strange relationship the three little heifer calves seemed to have. They never separated by more than a few feet and would group as if they had to have a conference whenever some strange new experience would crop up. He first showed me this behavior one day when we were out driving in the pasture to evaluate some sick calves. One of the triplets the one called Molly had a bad case of scours a.k.a. diarrhea. Normally when you drive through a group of calves the healthy ones will follow their mothers and get out of the way with no thought to the sick ones that can't move as fast. Not so the triplets, even though the mother cow headed out assuming the group would follow the two healthy calves would not leave Molly and did the strange grouping conference that was to become so familiar with them. Putting their heads together they seemed to be talking things over as we drove up and even when we caught Molly and were giving her fluids and antibiotics, the other two stayed close to watch and confirm that we knew what we were doing.

As the weeks and months slipped by, the three little calves grew like weeds and continued their close relationship. I saw them several times during the summer, always together and always keeping track of each other until fall came and weaning time arrived. As we worked the calves, giving shots, worming, etc, we noticed that all three heifers stayed together in the catch pen never getting out of touch with one another until finally one of the heifers was forced to come down the alley by herself. The other two reluctantly held back. After we had finished with the first, the strangest thing happened. The heifer, I think it was Bertha, ran back to the catch pen on the outside next to the working alley. An unbelievable response from a scared calf. Sticking her head through the bars of the pen, she had a conference with the other two and wouldn't you know it, both heifers seem to have been told, "Hey girls, it's not so bad. You can handle it." They both headed down the alley without any prodding or encouragement from the cowboys, quietly waited their turn and let us do our thing. When the trio was again united outside, they had one of their now famous conferences with their heads together for a few minutes then quickly went about their business.

As the years went by, the heifers became mature cows and had calves of their own but the relationship never changed. All three could be found together with their calves in tow during the summer months on pasture and would line up at the feed bunk in the winter being warmed by each others touch as they ate their silage. Every year during pregnancy testing, the three always came down the alley together one right after the other and continued their little chats afterwards.

When the cows were ten years old, the three soul mates faced their severest challenge. Curt called me out in June just a few weeks after turn out to assist him with a bad case of foot rot. It was Molly. She could barely walk her left hind hoof hurt so bad. The foot was swollen to three times its normal size and the pus oozed out the top of the hoof. As usual all three triplets were together, this time in a small valley lush with grass, with a small pond in the center, a perfect place to be for a bedridden cow. We easily caught the dead-lame Molly and treated her the best we could. It didn't look good. An infection this severe can be the end of a cow. For three weeks the threesome never left the little valley and with their calves the other two cows worked with Molly on a daily basis, making her get up and graze when all she wanted to do was lay down and give up. Several times I visited the little group, more to watch their interactions than to help Molly.

Once the infection was under control about all you can do is let nature take its course and hope the hoof heals itself well enough for the animal to again get around and feed herself. Finally, the badly damaged foot began to heal but not before Molly had lost about 400 pounds and looked like a dried-up pile of bones and hide. The other two never gave up the ship and continued to give her what seemed to be moral support all that summer. Often you would see the three lying, chewing their cuds with their heads inches apart, ruminating on the unfairness of life on the prairie with a sore foot.

By fall it was apparent Molly was going to live but with all the problems of the summer she hadn't settled with calf. She was open at pregnancy testing time. As I put an orange O on her hip so Curt could cut her out later to haul to the sale barn, it hit me. How could anyone separate these three? Curt was having the same thoughts, but how could a rock hard 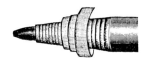 rancher keep an open cow for sentimental reasons? She was a financial drain that normally wouldn't be tolerated.

He tried to make light of it. "Looks like the three musketeers will have to get broken up this year. Wonder what they'll have to say to each other about that?"

Just like every other year the three were now standing together having just been reunited and seemed to be talking the whole thing over. I couldn't imagine him selling one of them.

He went on. "Guess there's no hurry about hauling her off though. We should put a little weight on her bones first. Maybe I'll haul her in around Christmas or so."

Just as I expected Christmas came and went and Molly was still with the herd. In fact spring came and I couldn't resist asking him about the free boarder.

"Hey Curt," I began, "When are you going to get your money out of that Molly cow? It's past Easter now. Which Christmas did you mean anyway?"

"I'm afraid she's just a little too thin yet to bring a good price. Maybe I'll just keep her until after calving and get some more flesh on her."

That summer at turn out time the three sisters all went out the gate together and Curt had his usual lame excuse.

"She'll pick up a little on pasture this summer and we'll let her go next fall."

"Curt," I reminded him, "By fall she'll be bred again and you will have lost the whole season so you may as well keep her another year if she's pregnant."

His eyes lit up with a mischievous shine, "Yeah, guess that's right I never thought of that. Well, the other two should be happy anyway."

It didn't work out that way. Curt called early one morning in August after a particularly rough thunder storm the night before with the bad news.

"Can you come out this morning, Doc.? We had a disaster last night and I lost some cows to lightning."

I imagined his voice broke a little as he finished but maybe it was my phone playing tricks.

It was a disaster all right. The triplets had been standing together as always near a big cottonwood tree with the two calves snuggled in between for warmth. The bolt had come down the tree and grounded within a few feet of the entire bunch, all five were dead.

I could see Curt was really shook, so was I.

"Maybe this is best, Curt. At least you won't ever have to separate them and you'll still get your money from the insurance company. They were getting old and sooner or later you would have had to make some hard choices."

As he sat down on a big cottonwood stump, he waited a few minutes before he spoke, to clear his mind I'm sure.

"Be honest, Doc. What do you really think they were doing when they used to have conferences?"

"I don't know, Curt. I've thought about it for years and just don't know."

We sat together for several minutes lost in our own thoughts. Did they communicate? Did they have feelings for each other? Did they reason?

Most scientists will tell us the answer would have to be in the negative but most scientists never met Molly, Helen, and Bertha.

Cows Have Miracles If You Watch For Them

Some of the worst situations veterinarians find themselves in often involve uterine prolapses. When a group of vets get to telling stories, you can almost bet several tales will involve middle of the night uteruses usually in big old Holstein cows.

There seems to be a rule that Holstein cows only calf at night and only push their uteruses out at 2 a.m. Perhaps they know more than we give them credit for about the nocturnal habits of human beings and are doing it just to get back at us for stealing their milk. A big calf can easily weigh around 120 lbs. so can you imagine the sack that must contain this baby inside the cow? Now imagine that same sack hanging outside the cow. It will be about three-feet long and weigh a good 150 lbs. It is your job, should you be fool enough to accept it, to push this entire bloody behemoth back through a hole that seems to be about the size of your fist. Meantime, the cow is usually struggling enough to throw you off just when you get started, time after time. Did I mention? You have to be very careful not to push your hand through the wall, nor to include too much dirt and manure with it even though it may be covered with mud, straw and other items I won't even discuss.

All in all uterine prolapses are one of the more challenging jobs we face out on the farm. One of my most memorable prolapses involved a big old red Angus cow, and strange as it might seem, I didn't even get out of the pickup. It started one beautiful spring day with a call from Dan Hebron. Even though it was in the middle of the afternoon, I knew trouble was imminent or at least very possible from the message.

now!

"Doc," said my secretary on the radio, "Can you go straight out to Dan's? He's got a uterus out and it sounds like a bad one. He can't get her in but says you can drive right up to her out in the pasture."

"Yeah, sure," was my sarcastic answer, "Then what, is he going to bulldog her when she takes off for the south eighty?"

She can be just as sarcastic, "No, but he said he'd let you rope her if you promised to be gentle."

Dan was one of my favorite people, a big kid that had passed the forty mark several years ago but still thought he was twenty-one. He was under the illusion that he was going to be a cowboy when he grew up. I had to hand it to him though, he sure could rope. Dan would drive a hundred miles for a jackpot roping contest just to see if he could get lucky and win fifty bucks. Once, when a calf managed to slip through the chute on us, he had jumped on his horse, that was always tied nearby (just in case he got lucky and something like this happened), and had roped and drug the little bugger back to the holding pen before it had gone a hundred yards. He'd use any excuse to practice his roping. Once he claimed he had even roped a coyote, but that would be another story.

Like most of the cowboy types, Dan was forever breaking in a new colt, and this one was always going to be the "Perfect Horse," the big money winner. That was what caused most of our problems.

As I drove into the yard, Dan was ready and mounted, "We'll just drive out to her, Doc and if she does get up, I'll snag her for you a minute. Follow me."

Dan on his colt and our strange pickup were all it took. By the time we got in sight, the cow was up and spooked. Her eyeballs were as big as saucers and her ears up. This old cow wasn't taking no crap off of anybody.

"You sure you got enough horse under you to handle that old rip?" was my casual question as Dan prepared his lariat.

He was very insulted. "Hey, this little bugger is going to be the best roper I ever owned. All he needs is a little practice, Doc."

My point precisely.

With that, the two of them were off to chase down my patient. It turned out there wasn't much chasing involved. It was more like the chaser became the chasee. It's quite easy to rope a cow when she obediently sticks her head under your horse trying to tip you over. Getting the noose around her neck was the easy part. The trouble started when she realized what had happened. That old red cow decided it was time to head for greener pastures, and thirty feet of lariat is enough to get up quite a head of steam if you're mad enough. A big mature experienced horse might have handled it. Dan's colt didn't have a chance.

It seemed like the whole world was suddenly rolling. The cow did a complete loop; Dan and the colt did a complete loop; the dust flew. This part actually turned out pretty good. As the dust cleared, I could see Dan sitting on the prairie, shaken, but by some miracle, not hurt. The cow and the colt were standing glaring at each other the length of the rope apart, and I had a big problem. My patient wasn't cooperating very well.

Once again the old cow decided it was time to get the heck out of there. She took off. The colt tied to her had little choice. He more or less followed along, keeping the full thirty feet away as much as possible.

It was about this time the cow discovered something else was going on. She noticed this giant sack of uterus hanging down behind, knocking on her legs and suddenly scaring the daylights out of her. The last we saw of the pair they were headed over the hill, the cow bucking and snorting and the horse making a slow big circle around her as he galloped trying his best to stay out of her way.

With a sheepish look on his face, Dan got in beside me with a brilliant observation, "Guess I didn't have enough horse, Doc. What are we going to do now?"

"Darned if I know. She'll probably be dead before long anyway. These prolapses can't take a lot of messing."

"Yeah, I know. Well, let's follow along and see if we get lucky. Maybe I can get back on the horse and figure out a way of controlling her."

I had to hand it to Dan. He had guts to even think of getting back on that horse. About fifteen minutes later we again caught sight of our missing duo. We could see them standing and glaring at each other about a quarter of a mile away.

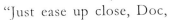

"Just ease up close, Doc, and I'll jump out and get on. Then we can somehow get her hog-tied."

Yeah, sure. The old red cow wasn't done yet. When she saw us coming, she quickly went back into action. Unfortunately, she had had time to rest up a little and was ready for some serious business. Just as she started to run the uterus banged her a good one in the hocks and it was like jabbing her with a prod. All concern about us vanished. She just started going, bucking and running. The colt, to his credit, stood his ground for a while – but it wasn't good for us. By the time the old cow had circled around the colt on the end of the rope, she ended up coming our direction. I saw disaster about 10 seconds before it hit. The colt lost his pull and decided he better run to catch up, so here they came straight at us with the rope stretched between. The cow went past on the passenger side and the colt went past on the driver's side. The rope just about cleared the hood but caught up on the grill. I've often wondered what that colt thought when he came around the back of my truck and met that old cow coming straight at him, just as they both ran out of rope. Inside the truck it felt like a 7.3 Richter earthquake as the two almost met. It seemed like the whole world was rolling again with the colt down on one side and the cow down on the other. We couldn't even get out of the truck, far less do anything. The rope was tight against both doors.

Dan with eyes as big as pie plates asked the obvious, "What ya gonna do now Doc?"

This time I had a plan and a darn good one. I reached out of the window and cut the rope with my jackknife.

"Doc, my God? That rope cost thirty bucks."

"Yeah, but my rear view mirrors cost a hundred bucks each and I've already lost one of them."

Our sparring partners were finally free of each other but my problem hadn't been solved. My patient was still not cooperating, still needed attention and was once again headed for parts unknown with her uterus flopping along behind. Mother nature, in her infinite wisdom, soon came to my rescue, however, and solved the problem for me.

As the old cow bucked her way over the hill we both gasped in astonishment as the uterus, with something like a whip lash effect was suddenly torn free and went sailing up in the air. It was like a slow motion movie as the bag went end over end twenty feet up and then back down to land with a thump in the grass.

Neither of us said a word for a few seconds as we contemplated what had happened.

Then Dan broke the silence, "Reckon we solved that problem, don't you think?"

"Yeah, we just ended up with one dead cow, that's for sure."

Philosophically he took the high road, "Well, we did the best we could. Maybe next time I'll make sure my horse is up to the job."

Always the optimist, I was just thinking if we could catch the old girl, maybe I could somehow get the stump pulled out and tie it off, and just possibly we could save her yet.

"You know, Dan, if we could catch the old rip we still might ...."

"Don't even think about it, Doc. She'll either live or die but there's no way I'm messing with her anymore. We have a broken rope, a bro-

76

ken mirror, several dents in your pickup and I'm starting to ache all over from being rolled in the dirt. Enough is enough."

I never saw Dan all summer and had pretty well forgotten the whole incident until that fall when I was out doing some herd work for him. As we were going through the cows pregnancy testing, worming, and pouring them for lice, I came on a big red cow that, search as I might, didn't seem to have a repro-

ductive track inside her. Even with cows that are not pregnant, you must feel the uterus and ovaries to determine for sure that there is not a calf inside. As I hunted in vain, I happened to look up and see Dan grinning like he really had an inside joke about something.

Finally he just couldn't hold it anymore. "If you find a calf in that old reprobate, you really are a miracle worker, Doc."

It hit me, "You mean....?"

"Yep, she never missed a beat. Raised a good calf, too. Guess she's just too ornery to die from a little old prolapse."

I couldn't argue with his logic.

Farm Kids Are A Little Different

I enjoy farm kids. They have a certain earthiness about them and a sophistication all their own. Their sophistication is completely different than their city cousins. It has to do with things like prolapses, sexual differences and func-tions, death, hard work, and a very easy sense of humor. Believe it or not, there are still kids out there who would rather rope calves than play Nintendo, who would rather catch frogs than steal hubcaps, and who would rather ride horses than roller blades. Most farm kids I've known think they're a little better than kids raised in town and that includes even the little towns of six or seven hundred people. In their eyes, kids that come from the big city are something to be pitied. After all how can you respect someone who has never been run over by a bucket calf or never seen a litter of pigs born.

One of my favorite families are the Dooleys. They kind of repre-sent what a farm family should be like. Wayne, the father, is a soft spoken young man who farms with his dad, works his tail off and is doing very well. He takes care of his business and sees to it things get done. His wife fits the picture like a glove. Sally takes care of the house, works in town part-time, raises the boys, helps with chores, and does whatever else she can find time for. I don't know how she manages it all. Their two boys are typical farm kids. Larry is twelve and never says a word until he gets to know you. Kevin is a little hell-raiser. He's eight and always instigating something.

As I drove into Dooley's yard, I could see this wasn't going to be a routine visit. Wayne had called with a few lumps to treat, which in itself was rather ordinary but the group standing by the barn waiting for me was obviously not. Wayne, Sally, and the two boys were their usual smiling selves but with them was a strange looking family, very out of place. The leader of the group was a man in his fifties who was perfectly round. He stood about 5' 6" and had a round belly, a round bald head, even his pudgy little hands seemed round. He was dressed in a pair of pure white Bermuda shorts which accented his round little knees and skinny legs. He had a flowery shirt, white socks, pure white tennis shoes, and a straw hat obviously bought just for this outing into the hinterlands. His eyes were concealed behind a pair of reflecting sunglasses. The mother was almost iden-tically dressed but was his exact opposite in physical appearance. She was at least twenty years his junior, tall and blonde. You could bet he had caught her with money, lots of it. The two kids, a boy and girl, looked so much like their parents it was uncanny. The boy was short and round about nine or ten years old, and the girl was tall and blonde about twelve years old. They were dressed exactly like their folks clear up to the reflector sunglasses. This group was so clean it was scary.

Wayne had been having a problem with lumps in his yearlings and this was the third time in the last few months that I had been out to take care of them. What we call lumps in cattle are actually abscesses under the jaw and upper part of the neck. They fill with a thick creamy exudate which must be drained and flushed out. The first time I had treated lumps had been quite an experience for the two boys who had become quite enamored with all that pus. It had started a game of "gross out" between the three of us. I was leading the game at this point but knew I better have my wits about me if I was to keep up with this pair.

As I stepped from my truck, the identity of the strange family was soon made clear. It seems they were visiting as part of a church exchange program between the local Lutherans and a large church in Minneapolis and would be staying for a week to see how the other half lived, so to speak. The father was Dr. James T. Armstrong, M.D., prominent thoracic surgeon and, believe it or not, he actually used the word prominent. He quickly enamored himself with me by starting a conversation.

"I understand you are going to do some surgeries today. Do you think it is wise to attempt surgical intervention under these primitive conditions? Haven't you people ever heard of hospitals?"

My mouth dropped open as I was caught speechless. Finally I managed to mutter, "Well, I guess I had just planned on draining some lumps."

"I've had a lot of experience in surgical technique and would like to help if you don't mind. Perhaps I could give you come pointers."

Starting to get my wits about me again, I introduced a little humor. "I'm always ready to learn new techniques. Maybe I should just watch."

About this time, the eight-year old came to my rescue. He was well organized and determined to win the game this day. As he handed me a quart jar, he said, "Hey Doc, you better catch some goodies so your wife can fix you some really good gravy tonight for a change."

My answer was so great it almost scared me, "Tell you what Kevin, I'll catch the jar full and we'll all have a nice warm drink of custard when we're done."

I can be a master at gross out with an eight year old. I was sure he flinched. Meanwhile the Armstrongs just didn't get it. They knew it was an inside joke and were already starting to resent not being the center of attention.

Dr. Armstrong decided he better put me in my place, "Can I carry your surgical pack for you? You do prepare sterile packs for these procedures, don't you?"

I was really starting to get sick of this guy.

Kevin, however, was just getting started as he pulled out a hamburger bun from deep inside his coat pocket.

"Maybe you should make yourself a quick pudding burger. I've even buttered it for you."

Wayne and Larry both turned a little green. This kid was good.

Mrs. Armstrong was starting to catch on and wasn't liking it one bit. She decided it was time to straighten out the yokels.

"Please," she said, "My children are not used to such vulgar talk and I would appreciate it if you two stopped right now."

I was chagrined. Kevin was elated. He knew victory was in sight. I frowned at him just enough to let him know we better knock it off before the little bugger got me in trouble but I knew this battle wasn't over. He looked way to smug for his own good.

Things went smoothly enough as I treated the first two calves. It is really quite simple, catch their head, inject some sodium iodine in the vein, and open the abscess. The first two had just small little lumps that contained nothing remarkable. The third one was a different story. The lump was large and tight as a drum. Kevin had been waiting for this one.

As I lanced the swollen jaw, the yellow exudate started rolling out, perhaps two quarts maybe more. I'm sure most medical doctors have seen pus, but I bet few of them have seen pus you can measure by the quart. The good Doctor Armstrong started it even before Kevin had his chance, just a slight gagging sound, almost undetectable. Kevin chose this moment to win the game. From inside his coat pocket the little bugger pulled two items, a table spoon and a plastic container of tapioca pudding. Noisily slurping the first bite, he very nonchalantly reached around me and filled the spoon with, you know what.

Several things happened all at once.

Wayne and Larry decided they had to check some cattle around behind the barn.

My stomach did several cartwheels but I'll never in a hundred years admit it to Kevin.

The Armstrongs, quite literally, lost it. If you have ever seen a cartoon of people on a ship all lined up along the rail you have the picture. There they stood leaning over the fence with their backs to us, all four perfect white butts in a row, all losing their breakfast. Kevin proclaimed himself the winner. I agreed.

The Armstrongs made a beeline for the house as soon as possible. Kevin and I finished the last two lumps and eventually Wayne showed up acting as if nothing had happened. I was feeling pretty bad about the whole affair as I cleaned up my tools.

"I'm sorry, Wayne," I said, "I guess I kinda let things get a little out of hand."

He never said a word as we watched the Armstrongs come out of the house suitcases in hand, load their car, and peel out of the yard. Now I really felt dumb. Sally exited the house next with a puzzled look on her face. Wayne met her half way to my truck and they stopped to talk. Had I just lost one of my best clients?

In a moment they turned my way, and boy, was I ever glad to see them both smile. Wayne was the first to speak.

"Doc, Kevin, thanks a million. We owe you guys one."

The Value Of Money

One of the most frustrating things about working with farmers and ranchers is the battle against money. It's hard to spend $200 on a sick calf that could be replaced at the local sale barn for $75. Over the years you learn to work within the limitations and it forces you to become very innovative at times. With small animals it's more a mat-

ter of values. Every dog owner in a rural community has a line you cannot cross when it comes to money. You learn early on there is a big difference between:

"We don't care what it costs Doc. Just do everything you can," and days later when it's all over and you present your bill to the following attitude: "Holy cow Doc! It's just a stupid dog. We could get a new one for free. Don't you think you're a little out of line?"

It's always fun to see what people can come up with next to get you to lower your bill or trick you into committing to something before you realize you've done it. I had an old Dutch farmer call me on the phone one day with a simple question.

"What do you charge to pregnancy test cows, Doc?"

Not suspecting anything unusual I gave a simple answer, "A dollar a head is the going rate these days."

"Well," he said, "That sounds pretty good. When can you come out and do some? Oh, you'll need to bring your chute. That isn't extra, is it?"

Still not suspecting anything, I hooked like a waterlogged catfish, "No, there's no extra charge. We could do them on Thursday afternoon. How many do you have?"

"I'm not sure how many we'll do. It depends on my son and whether he wants to do his. You know where I live, don't you?"

"No, I'm not sure I do. Have I been out before?"

"No, you haven't, I ain't had a vet on the place in ten years or so.

I'm not made of money, you know. To get here you go 15 miles east of town and 6 north, then take a right and go 5 more east. Well, we'll see you on Thursday, I guess."

"OK, but I'll need to get some idea on the number so I know about how long it will take and can schedule around it."

"Like I said I ain't sure but it should be either 3 or maybe four if the boy wants to do his."

I knew I had been gobbled up by a master. This guy was good.

"But you realize, don't you, Mr. Veurink, I can't drive 26 miles and set up my chute for 3 or 4 dollars? I'll have to charge a trip charge for a job that small."

"You said you charged a dollar a head. You going back on your word?"

Do you ever just lose it when you least expect it and say something all wrong? I do that once in a while.

"Mr. Veurink, I'd suggest you take your 3 cows and your son's one cow, wrap them in saran wrap and put them where the sun doesn't shine."

"You vets are all alike. You get to thinking you're just too independent for us small guys."

WHAM! went the receiver in my ear. It really hurt my feelings.

Probably the worse thing any farmer can say about the vet is, "He's getting independent." Every other farmer knows what that means without any explanation and will nod his head sagely whenever it is mentioned.

Another time I was accused of being independent came a few years later with another old Dutch farmer and a group of pigs that mysteriously kept changing numbers on me.

"Can you come out in the morning and vaccinate some pigs for me?" was the simple request.

"You bet." I answered. It was summer and work was as slow as it gets. "How many and what time?"

84

"There's 88 pigs and we should start around 7 a.m. before it gets hot. What do you charge by now?"

"I'm still getting 40 cents a pig and that hasn't gone up since pick-ups cost $6,000 back in '73. Guess it's about time to think about a little raise, don't you think?"

Humor often eludes an old Dutch farmer, "Sounds to me like it's went up about the same as the price of hogs."

He had me there. What could I say?

I suspected we had a problem when my syringe count went over 90 and there was still a good-sized pen to go. I thought I'd better start breaking the news to him right away.

"Looks like we'll have a few more than 88. Might even reach a hundred according to my syringe."

"You'd better check your syringe 'cause I know there are 88. I had eleven sows and they averaged 8 pigs a sow. That makes 88 unless they're multiplying."

Now he could find some humor even though it didn't seem funny to me. I never said another word as the count went over 100 and finally ended on 104.

As I cleaned up my syringe and prepared to leave, I gently broached the subject again.

"You sure you didn't have 13 sows in the bunch. My count came out at 104 which would be 13 at 8 pigs per sow. I'm sure that's the right count. The syringe came out at 104 and I used a 100 dose box of vaccine plus I opened a 5 dose to finish up. What do you think?"

"Well, I might have had 12 sows but I'm sure there wasn't 13. I suppose if you say so there must be 104. It's too late to count them now."

I never said another word. It was enough for him to admit he wasn't even sure how many sows he'd farrowed.

I didn't hear another word about the

pig count for many months. He paid the bill and I figured it was all over until one morning over a year later when he showed up at the clinic with a complaint.

"Say Doc," he started out. "Did I ever tell you? You were wrong about the count on those pigs you did the other day."

My mind was a complete blank. Try as I might I couldn't remember doing any pigs for him lately. This of course is a great trick to shorten up time. The other day can mean as long a time as you want it to while implying the transaction is still current and under consideration by all parties. Finally it dawned on me. He was talking about last

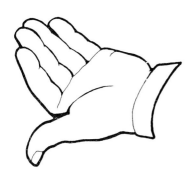

summer. My mouth fell open. Surely he didn't have the audacity to want a change now.

"When I sold those pigs last fall, the count was really 102. At least that's what I got paid for so that had to be what we did. I didn't lose any after that."

Normally I don't stutter a lot when I talk but this time I must have sounded like a broken typewriter as I tried to get an answer out.

"Wh.Wh.Wh.What do you want now after all this time?" was the best I could do.

"Well," he replied, "It seems to me like you owe me 80 cents."

I quickly reached in my pocket and pulled out three quarters and a nickel. I knew when I was beat. In the long run a professional will always win over an amateur no matter how hard the poor amateur tries.

Even after dealing with farmers that were real masters in squeezing every dime till it squealed it took a little old couple from back east to teach me the real meaning of humility in money matters.

Three sets of big brown eyes looked at me. Three thin bodies all angled with legs a little short for the trunk. The same questioning look was on all three faces. I had to start reading the chart before my sense of humor made me say something really dumb. Is it true that people that have been married long enough start looking alike? Or even more important does their dog start looking like them?

It had seemed like a routine appointment. Their dog had been a little sickly the last few days, probably nothing very serious, but who were these people? I lived in a town way too small to have characters like this trio that I didn't know. I knew everyone in town, yet here they stood. The duet of humans in this family consisted of a little man who stood about five foot tall with a frail little body and pure white hair. He wore a pair of wire glasses that perched on the end of a long narrow proboscis. His 1970's style suit coat and pink shirt were highlighted with a short wide tie that struggled to reach the shiny white plastic belt. This in turn accented his polyester slacks, waffled with brown and black stripes, that must have come from Good Will sometime in his youth.  To put it short he was a rather seedy little character completely out of place in small town South Dakota. The mate to this conspicuous little guy was his exact twin except she happened to be of the female gender and was wearing the feminine version of his 1970's attire: The same wire rimmed glasses, a yellow polyester pants suit, green scarf, and white plastic high heeled shoes.

The dog was a brown dachshund, greying at the muzzle with little dashes of misplaced white hairs bounding out around her eyes and ears, certainly not a purebred. She did not have the prominent spectacles that her two friends wore but the little plaid polyester coat she sported fulfilled the basic requirements of belonging to this eccentric family.

I could see why Sharon, my receptionist, had barely stifled her laughter when she told me two of my old high school buddies where in the exam room to see me.

"I'll get her," I quietly laughed to myself as I surveyed the three characters on and around my exam table. When I introduced myself, I discovered why I had never seen this trio before. They were just passing through town on the way to visit his sister in the Black Hills when Heidi had taken ill on the road. I had to chuckle at the quaint way they talked, probably from back east, I surmised.

The good humor quickly faded as I glanced at the card in my hand and the history Sharon had jotted down for me.

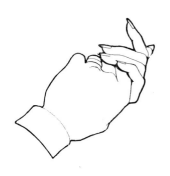

Name: Heidi

Age: 9 yrs.

Sex: Unspayed female

Breed: Dachshund

Reason for visit: Heidi has not been eating well, just mopes around. She seems to be getting a little bloated and won't play like she used to. She was in heat about three weeks ago.

My spirits continued to slide as I finished my workup, until the diagnosis was assured and the only thing left was to break the news. As gently and easily as I could, I gave them the story. Diagnosis – pyometra, which was very severe (and I stressed the severe) infection of the uterus. This syndrome happens to most older unspayed female dogs sooner or later. Prognosis – terrible, the infection had already gone too far and would be very hard to stop (and I stressed the very hard part). Treatment – surgery, about $100 worth (which was about half my usual fee for this terrible job). I noticed them both cringe when the $100 came out and wished that I'd said $50.

"Doctor," said the little man, "We know you will do the best job possible on our baby. She's all we have, you know?"

"Could you hold a check until the twentieth? That's when our social security comes. We don't receive very much but we get by," was the lady's inquiry even as her eyes begin to glisten with tears very near the surface.

"You can pay me whenever you want," was my feeble reply as I begin to feel less and less like a professional and more and more like Scrooge, Captain Hook and Jack the Ripper all thrown into one.

With tears now flowing freely, the little lady tried to ask another question which finally came out of the man. (*Perhaps they even use the same brain*, was the crazy thought going through my head as he finally blurted it out.) "Doctor! Is there any chance you might consider doing the job for a little less? It's been a really tight year for us," he exclaimed as both wrinkled cheeks became bathed with freely falling tears.

"I understand," was my almost tearful reply, "My grandmother has quite a time living on her Social Security too. I'll tell you what I'll do. If you can just pay me for the cost of some of the drugs, about $20, I'll donate my time to help you out. How would that be?"

I've had some tough pyometras in my day but that little Dachshund took the grand prize. Nothing seemed to go right. Veins too small for a decent catheter, uterus blown up like a sausage, blood everywhere. "What else could possibly go wrong?" I kept saying to myself as this nightmare surgery seemed to go on forever. My partner who was helping me wasn't much help. He kept muttering things about how much we should be charging for this nightmare and $200 just never was enough for one of these tough ones. I wisely kept my mouth shut.

Finished at last, dog still alive, I.V. dripping just like it's supposed to, breathing steady but labored. Maybe I better stay in the clinic a few hours tonight and keep an eye on things just in case.

The next few days were nip and tuck with the little man and his sidekick becoming daily visitors to check on things and make sure everything possible was being done for their baby. Several times I thought little Heidi was a goner but each time her will to live seemed stronger than her need to die and she would rally one more time. Finally on day five she showed some real life and I knew we had won the battle. I could count on one finger the number of pyometras this bad I had saved over the years.

"Hallelujah!" Boy am I feeling good. Heidi is up and at 'em, eating good, no fever, no discharge, I helped some people who really needed it. Life is good! Today she goes home as I joke with my partner and flirt with my receptionist. Man, am I in a good mood.

"We are so thankful for all your help, Doctor," states the little lady as I fairly beam at the family all looking at me with their big brown, now smiling eyes.

"Yes," said the little man, "It's so nice to find someone to help you when you are a long way from home. I don't know what we would have done without you."

"Now how much do we owe you, Doctor?" she asked, even as her voice trembled a little in fear of my answer.

"Oh shoot, you've been such a joy. Let's just call it even. I've had $20 worth of satisfaction working with such nice people," I replied as my partner started to frown a little from the exam room door where he was standing.

"Oh thank you so much, Doctor, but we didn't expect anything like that. You are so nice. I can't believe it," she stated as I glanced at

my partner and basked in the good will flowing my way.

"Come on! I'll help you to your car," I said, not wanting the moment to end.

After closing the car door and getting my little family all settled, a wave of doubts suddenly washed over me.

"Nice car you folks have here," was my feeble statement as my partner now openly frowning stood in the clinic door, obviously biting his tongue for the moment.

"Oh yes." said the little lady, "We bought it just after we got back from Europe this spring. It's new you know, Henry wanted to get a Cadillac but I insisted on a Mercedes. I just don't believe in cutting corners when you want something important."

One Tough Family

The entire family lived right on the edge. You had the feeling that at any moment they could all go bonkers and start hitting each other with two by fours. I was more than a little nervous out at the Fryar place. The father was Bob Fryar and he was the weirdest one of all. Perhaps the two boys, John and Paul, caught their instability from their dad. The mother, however, was so far out she needed a telescope to see left field. The daughter probably caught her idiosyncrasies from Mom. The daughter's name was Janet but the family called her Sister. In her milking duds she was as feminine as a linebacker for the Packers. The two boys never stopped in their desire to make dad look dumb, make Sister look dumber and most important make the local vet look like an absolute dolt. They often succeeded. The boys and Sister were not your usual high school kids living at home. They were all in their mid forties, never been married and never seemed to realize

there was an opposite sex. Unless you would consider a continuous stream of profanity and gross depictions some type of awareness of gender.

The first time I went out to the Fryar's was an eye opener. As I pulled into the yard, the entire clan was waiting by the windmill standing in a small circle as if something momentous was going to happen. Inside the circle was a very dead Holstein cow laying next to the water tank. I soon found out she had died during the night after having been perfectly normal at chore time the day before. It was just about dark now and I wondered if they had been standing there all day looking at her and waiting for the vet to come and make things right. My surmise was very near the truth.

Bob greeted me with the facts. "She died last night and I've been thinking all day wondering what happened. So we thought we'd git a professional opinion."

Paul chimed right in. "She was a kicking old rip. Probably died from being ornery. Acted a lot like Sister on a cold morning."

Sister taught me fifteen new words in about ten seconds as she described her loving brother. I kept my mouth shut.

Paul wasn't as circumspect. "Yeah Sis, she even looked like your....."

WHAP!!

Paul hadn't noticed the bucket of table scraps Sister had been delivering to the hogs when the dead cow scenario had brought her to the meeting. I was flabbergasted. She would have killed a normal person. Paul never flinched. In fact he never quit chuckling as he picked potato peelings out of his hair and wiped a bit of blood off his ear where the bucket had caught him. I kept my mouth shut.

I was to learn it would take a lot more than a bucket of slop on the head to hurt Paul Fryar.

It didn't take long to determine the demise of the "kicking old rip." As I opened up the cavity to search the intestines I noticed a large pus filled pocket and massive infection around the intestines and stomach. As I pulled out a piece of bailing wire about six inches long I told them of their bad luck.

"Looks like she swallowed some wire that penetrated her stomach wall and set up an infection. We call it hardware disease. It's quite common, see them all the time."

The entire group seemed quite enthralled by this whole procedure. They obviously had never heard of anything so crazy. Shaking their heads and deep in conversation, the two women headed for the house and the boys drifted off to the barn probably to think it through and decide if I knew what I was talking about.

A few minutes later as I was cleaning up my knife and talking to Bob, Sister came out of the house with a large silver pan and a knife of her own the size of a small machete.

She told her father of her plan. "Ma wants the liver for supper tonight if you think it's OK."

"Sounds good to me. Some fresh meat would taste good."

My stomach lurched so high my tonsils could feel the eruption coming like a volcano preparing for its big day. This surprised me because by this time my stomach and I had weathered some pretty tough situations together without any major outburst. A few rotten dead cows, some pus pockets as big as gallon jars, and several other things too gross to mention were all part of our shared history.

After several minutes of discussion with my internal time bomb I got it under control and stuttered a few words to the Fryars. "I, I, I, I think the infection would spoil the meat, don't you think?"

Both Fryars looked at me like I was the crazy one. I didn't think so but I was beginning to wonder.

Sister wasn't to be denied, with a flourish she wielded her machete and sliced a chunk of liver about the size of a football into her pan.

I drove home with a new awareness of how silly our laws concerning the processing of meat must seem to people in the real world. E. Coli just didn't seem so bad anymore.

I discovered the entire family had survived the gourmet liver when I arrived on the farm about three months later to vaccinate a few heifers for bangs. Paul, however. didn't seem to be his usual jovial self, he wouldn't even respond to Sister's taunts when she accused

him of being lazy and shiftless. I just couldn't figure it out. Surely food poisoning wouldn't last this long. After the boys had caught and held about six heifers for me, I noticed a dirty white rag wrapped around Paul's index finger on his right hand. Looking closer, I noticed little red chutes of blood poisoning slipping out from under the rag and working their way up his hand. The hand was badly infected and needed some attention before he became really sick. I gently broached the subject.

"Looks like a mean sore you have there, Paul. Have you had a doctor look at it?"

His face turned red and a string of profanity expelled from his lungs. I had hit a sore spot, much worse than his finger.

"It's Sister's fault – the whole thing! I should have never listened to her. She's dumb as a load of rocks, you know."

Sister had to respond to so obvious a challenge. "Anybody stupid enough to use his finger for a plug better not be calling other people dumb."

I figured I better cool things down before the violence started. "What the heck did you try to plug up, a meat grinder?"

"No, it wasn't no meat grinder. How dumb do you think I am anyway?"

Sister continued, "He watches too many cartoons, can't tell real from made up, that's really blockheaded."

My curiosity was piqued, I had to explore further. "Tell me, Sister, what the heck did you dare him to do. You must have talked him in to something not very bright."

Paul just about choked. Sister continued. "Last Sunday morning we were watching cartoons on TV, you see. Well, Elmer Fudd was trying to shoot the rabbit but the rabbit was too smart. He stuck a finger in the end of the barrel and stopped the bullet. The barrel got big and exploded, but the rabbit was OK. All I did was dare this moron to try it and see how tough he really is. He thinks he's so tough you know."

"You mean he actually put his finger over the end of a gun barrel and pulled the trigger?"

"No, no, no, he's too big of a wienie to do that. I had to pull the trigger. He's just lucky I grabbed the twenty-two. If I had brought out the 30-30 he wouldn't have even slowed it down."

For the first and last time in what would become many years of working together, I saw Sister smile. In fact she even laughed a little just remembering the satisfaction of the entire adventure.

Paul had missed all the humor with his bad attitude. Why I could even muster a little chuckle thinking of the look that must have been on his face as his finger came away a half-inch shorter.

"Well, at any rate I think you need to head into town and see the doctor. You'll need some Penicillin or something before you get gangrene and they have to cut off the rest of your finger or your hand."

This instantly caught the attention of Bob. These were the words he wanted to hear. "You think a little penicillin would improve his attitude, Doc.?"

"I don't know. That would be up to the doctor I don't work on humans unless it's myself and I can't do any harm."

"Yeah, but you got penicillin, don't you?"

"Don't even think about it. You get this boy to a doctor as quick as you can before he really gets sick."

He didn't hear a word I said. "Well, what's the difference between your penicillin and the expensive stuff they have?"

"I'm sure it's about the same but you need some real help here and I'm not about to start giving farmers shots of any kind. They'd take my license so fast I'd be out of business before sunset."

"I have a bottle I bought from the feed store. S'pose that would be the same?"

I made the mistake of hesitating for a second and he knew he'd found his answer.

"How about a little needle Doc? All I have are cow needles and they might be a bit big for this critter."

Horses Are Only Human

Every small town has "The Horse Guy." The horse guy is usually a wizened little fellow who runs a half dozen mares and raises four or five colts a year. His main claim to fame is his ability to verbalize with absolute certainty on everything equine. The most amazing thing about the horse guy is his talent at getting people to hang on his every word. It's a wondrous experience to watch normal, logical, rational human beings swallow some absurd proclamation from the horse guy. Once I watched an entire room of people nod their heads in understanding and worship as

the horse guy emphatically, (as always) stated, "I'd never vaccinate any of my horses. It just causes them to go off their water, and that usually ruins a good horse."

Look out if you're a young vet and haven't learned the ropes yet. The natural inclination is to get into a discourse on medical procedures with the horse guy. Big mistake, he will always win. If you're foolish enough to open your big mouth as I was, he will eat you alive. In my young naive way I quickly found words to show my disapproval.

"That's crazy, it's been shown again and again that vaccination doesn't cause any harm and it's certainly better than letting them die from encephalitis. What do you mean by going off water anyway. Do you mean they can't urinate or what?"

Now the horse guy is in horse heaven. He has found a sucker.

"If you stay around here very long, you'll get to see a lot of horses off water, boy. Why one spring alone I treated off water horses every day for six weeks. Yep, it's really common around here."

"Yes," I still hadn't caught on, "but what exactly is wrong with these horses you're treating?"

"Well, a horse that can't pass his water is a completely different thing as you'll soon find out. I have a sure-fire cure for those buggers. Stop out some time and I'll fix you up with some drench. Oh, by the way around these parts we call 'em water bellies. Surprised they didn't teach you that in college."

This brings a small snicker from the crowd of now completely absorbed onlookers. The whole situation is starting to get interesting.

"Off water is not a specific diagnosis in anybody's book. Just what symptoms are these horses showing?"

"Holy cow don't they teach you kids anything these days? Even my Dad knew how to handle off water horses. Tell you what I'll do. Some evening when you aren't busy, why don't you just stop out and I'll go over a few of the basic horse problems with you. If you're not too stubborn to learn a few things from the school of hard knocks, I could really help you out."

Finally it's starting to dawn in my thick skull. I'm way out of my league. This guy is a master. I could talk all night and he would never give me even a smell of anything specific that I could really refute. My retreat is more than a little ignominious as I mutter, "Well all I know is you have to make a specific diagnosis before you can get good results."

"Oh, I can get results all right, but the best bet is still to stay away from these here vaccines so you don't have the problem to begin with."

I slunk home in disgrace, but much wiser.

My particular horse guy is named Alfred Leplatt and we have had our altercations over the years. I hate to admit it but he just about always manages to come out on top psychologically. From time to time he even has had to bite the bullet and ask for my help when things got out of hand out on his humble spread. Alfred is a little short guy at about 5' 4" with a bushy red beard surrounding a pair of bright blue darting eyes. His method of handling the world is to let his bluster lead the way and then negotiate with anyone not overwhelmed by his vocabulary of swear words, loudness and in-your-face belligerence. Like most people who really love horses, he is a pussy cat at heart and immediately wilts when challenged. Alfred nearly always wears a pair of filthy leather chaps, spurs, and an old felt hat badly in need of being thrown in the sanitary land-fill. His leather gloves are a constant companion. I suppose he never knows when an upstart young veterinarian will show up and need to be taken down a peg or two.

One of my first encounters with Alfred occurred one day when I was in the back of the clinic doing a Caesarian on a heifer. Sharon stuck her head through the door and asked if I could get the phone a minute. It seemed Alfred had a mare that was in heat continuously and had a question about some medicine. It's impossible to answer the phone in the middle of surgery. That, however, wasn't the answer he was looking for. Try as I might I hadn't had any luck reaching him back. The phone rang to a deaf ear all that evening. He was probably out trying to intimidate some young feed salesman in the pool hall. Early the next day I was in my office when I heard a commotion out front. Alfred blasted through the front door and his first words were, "@#%&#)(& AND *%)(*@# AND)*%½$# that young *%&½#)*."

I've always figured a good defense is a good offense so out of my office I came with my mirrored answer. "@#$*½)$% AND *%&#)*$ AND @&#(*$%, you old goat."

The pussy cat suddenly appeared. It was obvious he had thought I wasn't around.

"I just needed to ask a couple of questions. You vets get to thinking you're too good to talk on the phone to us common people."

"Alfred," was my quick reply, "You old fart, you know darn well I'll talk to you on the phone whenever I can. Now what's your problem?"

For the first time Alfred and I had a meaningful conversation about a sick horse. It was a good feeling but even better was the realization that I had stumbled onto the best way to handle the horse guy. You had to give it back faster than he could put it out and never, never show any sign of uncertainty or weakness. After that day we still had our little problems but all in all we have managed to keep our relationship on a pretty even keel after I taught him how to treat me.

Probably my most memorable case with the horse guy happened one hot summer evening. Temperature at 9 p.m. was still in the nineties when the phone rang and Alfred, without a hello, made one of his blunt statements.

"I need you right now. My stud is sick and it don't look good. How soon can you get here?"

I was enjoying the beauty of the evening on the drive out. This didn't sound too difficult, probably just a little bellyache. I should have known better. The horse guy would never let the vet have an easy one. It was completely dark by the time I drove up to Alfred's barn and let my pickup lights shine into the sorry looking stable. Alfred stood by the door with a worried look on his face and for once seemed a little humbled.

"He's sure acting strange, Doc. Never saw anything like it. Must need a tonic or something. What do you think it could be?"

"I don't know. Maybe we better have a look before we try to make a diagnosis."

"Yeah sure, he's in the barn here, but I'm afraid there ain't no lights. Just leave your pickup lights on an you can see just fine."

With that I stepped through the door which was about four feet wide, into a long narrow portion of the barn which had been added on years after the original structure. The pickup lights just weren't adequate and of course I had misplaced my flashlight. To top it off the horse was pure black

and seemed to be swallowed up in the inky darkness at the other end of the lean. As I stood about six feet inside the door, the hair on my neck began to stand on end. Something was terribly wrong. A noise started back in the darkness and slowly grew louder. It could best be described as though someone was typing on an old hand typewriter. Whoever was typing must have been a good student as he seemed to be getting better and better as the clicking became faster and faster.

It seemed like an eternity that I stood there but it was probably only about five seconds until my eyes started to adjust to the dim light. Slowly the black shape took form and I could see the stud standing at the far end. He was very much aware of me. The 1200 pound animal was glaring at me with his head about eighteen inches off the ground, ears laid back flat, the head resembled a snake as it weaved back and forth never once taking his eyes off me. It now become apparent what the strange noise was. The horse was gnashing and clicking his teeth as his powerful jaws went up and down.

I felt the movement as much as I saw it. He was coming! It took about two steps for the stud to reach full speed. The last thing I saw was the head going up and down, teeth still chattering. This was one of the few times in my life when I knew an animal really wanted to kill me and had no fear of the powers of man. The episode was in slow motion as I turned to flee and my feet were full of lead as I dove for the open door.

"CLOSE THE DOOR!" I shouted as I flung myself out into the warm night air. I was about as scared as I ever get. As I rolled into the

yard, Alfred, to his credit, slammed the heavy plank door in the stud's face. A half second later the door became kindling wood as the black never even slowed down. Boards, hinges, latch, and horse erupted on top of me. Someone was watching over me that night, not even a scratch. The horse didn't even see me as he escaped into the night. I did get to see a hoof that seemed as large as a pie plate tear out some sod eight inches from my head.

Alfred and I both had the same thought: He might come back. We jumped for the pickup and slammed both doors simultaneously. It took several minutes for my hands and knees to quit shaking. Alfred was the first to speak.

"What do you think is wrong with him, Doc?"

I have always thought my answer was a little inspired, "I don't know Alfred. My examination just didn't last long enough. I didn't even get his vital signs measured."

My humor was lost on him. "What are you going to do now. Think you can catch him?"

"Are you nuts, Alfred? What we're going to do now is wait till daylight and then take a look. I might be a little dumb but I ain't stupid enough to go after that thing again tonight."

All night I lay awake wondering what my plan of action should be come morning and reliving those few seconds when disaster was so close. Even now years later I can still feel the fear of those few seconds and wonder what would have happened if the black would have caught me.

The next morning I arrived on the farm just in time to watch Alfred drag the dead horse up by the silage pile for the rendering truck to pick up. "Whatever was wrong must have been rather serious," was my first thought, as I breathed a sigh of relief.

Several days later with the lab report in hand, I called Alfred to give him the news. By this time any humbling he had undergone that night had completely vanished.

"Looks like that stud had rabies, Alfred. We're really lucky neither one of us got exposed in all the ruckus."

His answer was very emphatic as usual.

"I don't think so. I've seen a lot of rabid animals and they sure don't act like that."

101

"Well, at any rate the test was positive and it's a very sure test. He sure acted like a rabid horse to me."

"Well, I know it wasn't rabies, but you can believe what you want I suppose."

Did you ever want to hit someone with a 2x4 just to get his attention?

The end of the rabid horse episode, as I started calling it, came about a week later in the local cafe one morning. I was sitting with a couple of guys having coffee when Alfred showed up with one of his buddies and sat at the next booth over. They didn't notice me when they came in and couldn't see me from where they sat. Unfortunately I could hear their every word. I cringed as I heard myself mentioned.

"Yep," Alfred was saying, "The stud is dead, best stud I ever had. I called that vet but just wasted my money."

"You're kidding," was his friend's reply, "What happened?"

"Oh, he thought it was rabid, seemed to be scared to death of the poor old bugger. I would have treated him myself, but I happened to be out of drench."

"Yeah, if you want something done right you have to do it yourself. What was wrong with him anyway?"

"The old guy was just off his water a little. I learned one thing, I'll never get caught without drench again."

Buttercup

Although I've seen many animals die, it never gets easy and I never seem to get any closer to understanding the process. That magical thing called life can slip away so easily. But other times it disappears only after the greatest of struggles. Many times it seems like a physical entity when you are trying so hard, pleading for it to stay even though you know it's probably leaving to wherever it goes, to be replaced by that other persona called death. I have a personal hatred of death. It seems like he's always lurking around waiting for some unfortunate puppy to screw up and allow him to mess up its chance to become a dog. Little puppies don't ask much out of this world, just a few good meals, something to chew on, and one real friend. The most endearing quality of any animal is their ability to live in the now. They never worry about the past and certainly don't care to fret about the future and the champions of living-in-the-now are puppies. A puppy lives for what's happening this moment in time, one hundred percent. Perhaps that's why I feel so responsible for a hurt or sick puppy, much more so than any other animal. It's hard to watch death incarcerate an innocent puppy especially one that is well loved, but sometimes it just happens.

The group that stood around the exam table was rather typical. A young couple with three little kids, one still being held by the mother and the other two just tall enough to see over the top if they stood on tip toe. Curt, the father, worked for the local co-op, pumping gas, changing tires, fixing lawn mowers, and various other duties. Judy, the young mom, was an old fashioned, stay-at-home mom, and take care of the kids. It was a big day for this young family, their first puppy, her name was Buttercup and she fit the part to a tee. Buttercup was a fine little cross bred collie/shepherd about 2 months old and so friendly she couldn't stop wiggling long enough for me to hear her little heart.

103

After much laughter and messing around the physical was done, the shot over, with all the kids having to look the other way, shots are awful when you're five years old. The perfect pet for the perfect family, I felt great as the little group made their way out of the office, this was the reason I went to Veterinary school.

I saw Buttercup several times over the next few weeks, once to give her a rabies shot and her booster for distemper, several times just to answer questions and give moral support. It was easy to tell this little dog had become an important part of the family. The visits were always the same: the entire entourage would arrive, Curt would stand in the corner and beam, Judy would ask questions and the kids would take turns trying to stump me with their insightful observations and questions. I love polite kids and have always wondered how some parents do it, a conversation might go something like this.

"Doctor, why do you put the thermometer in her poo-poo?"

"Oh just because it's handy."

"Doctor, why do you wash your hands so much. Is Buttercup dirty?"

"No, but I might have a rare disease I caught in the jungles of Africa and I wouldn't want her catching it, would you?"

"Doctor, will Buttercup have babies pretty soon?"

"No, she's just a baby herself yet."

"But are there any babies inside her?"

"Probably not but if there are we'll add a chapter to the Bible."

"Doctor, are you going to hurt her?"

"Not unless she bites me first, I always bite back."

On and on it would go, kids have a way of keeping you on your toes.

The first really big crisis came when Buttercup was six months old. It started with the phone about nine o'clock one evening when Judy called sounding very anxious.

"It's Buttercup, Doctor. We just can't figure out if something is wrong or not. She's acting so strange. Maybe she ate something that didn't agree with her."

"Could be. Tell me what she's doing."

"Well, she just seems so restless. She paces from window to door and back again. She doesn't seem to want to eat much and she's just not herself. Could you see her first thing in the morning?"

Although I was sure I knew the problem, it seemed to be a good idea to take a look just in case. This had gotten to be a very important dog in my life.

"Of course, Judy, why don't you stop by around nine or so and we'll have a look. I doubt if it's anything to serious. You guys try not to worry, OK?"

Sure enough, as the group filed into the exam room the next morning with worried faces all around, I saw the telltale straw colored fluid. Buttercup was in heat. How do you explain this phenomena of nature to two little kids? It's easy, you let the parents do it, unless they're too chicken.

I started the conversation as gently as I could, "I guess we're not in too much trouble. She appears to be coming into season. We should

have gotten that spay done a little quicker but no harm done. We'll do it just as soon as she gets through her cycle. Not many dogs come in this young. She's still just a puppy herself."

Boy, did that open a can of worms. The six year old immediately jumped straight to the heart of the matter.

"What season?"

I made a big mistake with the first answer that popped into my nervous grey matter.

"You see Buttercup is thinking about having a family someday and she's looking for a father. It's a very normal thing for a dog her age."

"Why does she need a father?" from the five year old.

"What does the father do?" asked the six year old.

I looked at Judy with a pleading expression. No help there, she was busy looking at the floor. Curt was having a hard time finding a lost item in his shirt pocket and must not have heard any of this. I knew I had to make a bold move. This wasn't the time to be timid.

Looking both kids in the eye I became very stern and in my gruffest voice I declared, "You guys will just have to wait till you get home and your mother will explain it all to you."

Without catching my breath so they couldn't interrupt I continued, "Just take her home and she'll be OK in a week or so, see you."

Out the door I went, the last thing I heard as I went down the hall was Judy in an accusatory voice hollering at me, "Thanks a lot Doc. You big wiener."

I hid in the back room until I heard their car leave, after all even veterinarians have their limits.

Disaster struck about two weeks later. I was on my way to town about 5 p.m. when my secretary called on the two-way with the disturbing message.

"You better hurry. Buttercup is here and it looks bad."

It was one of those all too frequent mishaps. Curt had been spreading some insecticide on the grass in the backyard with an insecticide stick trying to cut down on the mosquito population when he had been called to the phone. Without thinking he had left the three foot impregnated wax stick laying on the lawn. Buttercup had thought it a wonderful toy and had chewed the end off in a matter of minutes and swallowed it. Insecticide poisoning, quite common and quite lethal, about the only halfway good news was that it had a fairly good antidote if the exposure wasn't too severe. As I neared town, I started visualizing the best. Maybe it helps. I can never decide for sure, at least it never hurts to try.

As I entered the exam room, all eyes turned to me pleading for some good news, I struggled to find some. The heartbeat was slow and muffled, skin as pale as a sheet of paper, eyes dilated. I went into action as fast as possible, maybe a miracle would pull us out.

"Perhaps it would be best if you waited outside. I need to get an I.V. going and try to reverse the symptoms. I'll let you know as soon as I have any idea what we've got."

As the little group filtered out into the waiting room, I knew the chances of anything good were mighty slim. After I'd done all I could for the moment – an I.V. dripping, atropine as an antidote, and a heating pad for warmth – I went out to talk with the little family, to start preparing them for the inevitable.

"Maybe it would be best if you guys went on home. It looks really bad but I'll do what I can and we can hope for the best."

Judy was the first to speak.

"Would it be best if we said our good-byes now, do you think?"

"Yes, I think it would. Our chances are really grim."

I never believe in giving false hope when none really exists. When you do, it often comes back to haunt you after the wreck comes down. It was one of the toughest partings I've ever had the misfortune of witnessing. There wasn't a dry eye in the room when they finally headed home to an empty house.

All night long I stayed with Buttercup. She wasn't about to let death come easy. He was going to have to earn anything he got this

night. About 2 a.m. she quit breathing for a moment and again at 4:30 she almost stopped but both times I managed to pull her back into this world with I.V. atropine. Finally around six I decided to get an hour or two of shut-eye. She seemed to be about the same as when they had brought her in, no better and no worse, but I knew I was fighting a losing battle.

The phone jerked me out of a bad dream about 7:30. It was Judy. Those waiting room couches are sure hard and uncomfortable. I was stiff and sore all over plus a splitting-lack-of-sleep headache was settling in.

"We couldn't wait any longer, Doc. How's she doing?"

Guilt hit me like a sledge hammer.

"Can I call you right back, Judy? I need to check on her a minute before I say too much OK?"

One of the longest walks of my life was across the waiting room into the surgery to look in the cage. Nothing had changed, still breathing but barely. I felt like a winner. Life was still here. More atropine, more long hours of waiting and watching. Little Buttercup was one tough little dog.

The end of the battle came at 12:32 p.m. For some reason I looked at the clock and it stuck in my head, after all it was one of the most satisfying moments I ever had in practice. Buttercup raised her head and looked me in the eye very aware of her surroundings. I knew we had won this one. Death would just have to go find someone else to aggravate.

Real Men Are Tougher Than Cows

There is always a little danger involved when working cattle. Every farmer, rancher, and veterinarian can tell stories about broken bones, skinned knuckles, displaced fingers and a myriad of other bruises, aches and pains that they have received from some cantankerous old cow. I've received more than my fair share of bumps and grinds mostly because of a certain stubborn streak running through my ego. That is not a good thing. Which would you rather have, a little respect or a couple of broken ribs? Only an idiot would take the ribs but several times I have caught myself picking the wrong option. A twenty-year-old cowboy has about as much respect for his own body

as he does for the typical barn cat so why wouldn't he expect Doc to live on the edge also? After all if he's ready to jump on any half broke colt and ride him until the cowboy's either on the ground getting stomped or the colt is subdued, why shouldn't Doc be ready to jump into a pen with an old cow on the prod, tie her to a post and give her an I.V.?

One of the favorite exclamations when the going gets a little hairy is, "What's the matter, Doc? You ain't afraid of a little cow, are you?"

This, of course, is a direct challenge to any imbecile's manhood. It's akin to being called a sissy or a whoosh. Sometimes it seems like a person just can't resist taking the challenge. Getting hurt is invariably my own fault.

It's always a surprise how fast bad things can happen when the time is right. One minute you're whistling a tune, merrily lancing an abscess or wrapping a bandage and the next you're sucking a crushed finger and exclaiming to the world your opinion of all creatures great and small.

Usually it's the near misses that we talk about the most and that live in our memories for the longest time. The times when we almost really get it but escape unscathed to screw up another day.

The Forsythe ranch was a real ranch. It was so ranchy the hired hands were still wearing chaps to breakfast, and I suspect they slept in their spurs. Even the owner Old Harold Forsythe believed anything you  couldn't do on a horse wasn't worth doing. He was a big man, weighing around 250 pounds and it looked like he could bench press 400 pounds even though he was in his mid sixties when I first met him. He invariably wore a mammoth black hat, leather chaps, leather vest, and spurs as big as silver dollars. He sported a handle bar mustache that cleared his quick grin by at least four inches on each side, sideburns down to his prominent mandible and a red plaid hanky surrounded a bull neck of twenty-five inches. You wouldn't mess with Harold on Saturday night in the pool hall. He took no guff. The Forsythe ranch was a hard-working, hard-drinking cattle ranch with about ten cowboys on the payroll and over a thousand cows running the river breaks. It took a tough man to ramrod this crew. Harold, like most cow men, had a great sense of humor once he got to know and respect you but had nothing to say until you proved yourself in his eyes.

The first time I pulled into the yard and met this intimidating specimen, he was less than impressed I'm sure. It was a Sunday afternoon in early summer on what seemed like a rather easy situation, a routine calving call. I was soon to learn there would never be a routine call at the Forsythe ranch. His greeting was typical cowboy, "Who the hell are you?"

And before I could blubber out some inane answer he continued, "I called for the vet, not some kid still wet behind the ears."

The bad thing was he was right. You see I was out of school a full two weeks and knew about as much about pulling calves as his greenest cowboy. I did have the brashness of youth on my side which goes a long way when you're still too dumb to know what you don't know.

"I'm Dr. Wynia," I weakly mumbled, "I was told you had a calf to pull."

This great intellectual speech did a lot to lower my already lower-than-a-dog self image in face of this massive wall of doubt he was throwing my way.

"A little heavy on the Doctor for a kid, aren't you?"

Somehow I had to get this whole thing on a little more even keel. Boy, was I intimidated. My mouth felt as dry as a cup full of Borax.

Ignoring his put down, I took the initiative.

"You want me to work on her or you can wait for "The Boss," who will be back to work tomorrow?"

"You'll have to take it out the side. This one's too big to pull. Can you do that?"

"I guess we'll find out if we ever get started, won't we?" I was brash all right.

With this brilliant observation he headed for the calving shed with me rather meekly following along. The calf was a big one. I could see the rear legs which seemed to be the size of a yearling bull protruding from the nearly exhausted heifer. I really impressed this old hard core rancher with my brilliant observation.

"Looks too big to pull all right. Guess we better do a c. section."

He just glared in my general direction, not a word.

As I begin my prep, the cowboys started to wander in to watch the show. It didn't take them long to figure out this was my first Caesarian and they took full of advantage of my nerves.

"Did you ever save one before, Doc?"

"Hope you know which piece to cut in there, Doc?"

"What if she goes down and the guts fall out all over the barn. What you gonna do then, Doc?"

My hand actually shook as I pulled the scalpel down in one giant sweeping motion just as I was taught. Not a good idea 'cause my left hand was part of the long sweeping incision, what was I thinking of?

The cut in my thumb was an inch long and into the bone. I almost passed out right on the spot. After flooding the thumb with local anesthetic and wrapping a quick wrap, I had to carry on. What a nightmare. Everything that could go wrong did, of course. Just as I finished my opening, I got a wiff of rumen gas floating out of the cow. This was my first one but I knew something was bad wrong. Harold who was peering over my shoulder saw it before I did.

"Looks like you cut right into the stomach to me."

I never said a word but grabbed a needle and some catgut off the tray and started to suture. Here I was thirty minutes into the surgery and so far I had cut two things that hadn't needed cutting and wasn't much closer to the calf than when I started. That's when things really started going bad on me. The heifer did lay down and the intestines did roll out on the straw just as predicted. The long sweeping incision wasn't half long enough to get the calf out of so I had to stop in the middle and make it about five inches longer. The uterus was friable and wanted to tear with every suture. On and on. Blood everywhere. The cowboys even started to feel a little bit in awe of this whole thing, how could anyone screw up so much, so bad, so fast?

It was quiet in the shed as I put in the last suture and started cleaning up. All I wanted was to get the heck out of this terrible place and never come back. Harold spoke as I started my truck and took my last thread of self-esteem.

"I don't reckon we'll be paying for this one if she dies. You may need a little more practice before you try that again."

He didn't have a twinkle in his eye and wasn't grinning.

For the next week my thumb felt like it had been put through a meat grinder but I carried on the best I could. It helped matters a great deal when I learned the heifer had survived in spite of me and was doing fine.

The next time I was called to the Forsythe ranch, it was late fall, a cold rainy miserable day. I begged my boss, Dr. Holt, to let me off the hook and take the job himself, with no luck. His answer was the old cliche. "You get bucked off, you have to get back on and ride him again."

As I pulled into the yard, my chute rattling along behind I could see the whole crew was ready and waiting. About five cowboys and

Harold were perched on the fence. Harold's first words really put me at ease.

"How come the boss didn't come? I was expecting him."

Before I could answer he continued, "Why'd you bring a chute? We only have about a hundred to pregnancy test and sure don't need no chute."

Being completely without a clue I asked the obvious, "How do you plan on holding these cows without a chute?"

Six guys looked at me like I was a complete idiot. "Takes too long to catch each one. We just run them in the alley and you jump in behind the first one, do her, then climb up, let the next one come ahead, jump down again and do her, works great and goes a lot faster."

First impressions are usually the best. "Looks a little dangerous to me. What if the cow behind crowds in too tight and nails me? I think we better use the chute and do it right."

My manhood was immediately challenged, "You raised in the city somewhere or what? You won't make much of a vet if you're afraid of a few little old cows. Besides I'll have Bob here sit on the fence and keep those cows back until you're ready for them, easy as pie."

Looking at Bob convinced me I was in trouble but what can you do. If I didn't get in that alley now I would be branded for life. Bob was the stereotypical cowboy that hadn't made the grade. He had a five-day beard, dirty hair, front teeth long since gone to the tooth fairy, a dog-eat-dog grin that evinced a continuous alpha state and a hat so big it could be used for a circus tent. I knew from being a kid on the farm, the bigger the hat the more you better watch out: this guy may not be too competent.

The first few cows went rather easy and I was just starting to relax when the peppermint schnapps made its appearance. Nothing like a few shots of schnapps to make you feel better on a cold, wet day working cattle. Bob and I shared a pint or so as the next twenty cows went under me and it was surprising how much more humane and gentle a person old Bob became. I had just decided he was nearly my best friend in the whole world when it happened.

"Look out Doc, she's a rank one!" was Bob's near hysterical exclamation as I struggled with my arm as deep as I could reach inside a big old roan cow. I turned my head just in time to see the next cow, fire in her eyes, coming down the alley behind me. Nothing in the world was going to slow her down far less stop her, especially not one drunk cowboy with a two-foot stick in his hand. I did the only thing possible. I pulled my arm and hit the dirt. Or more aptly said I hit the cow manure, mud and various other body juices that come from cows when they are excited.

The next thing I saw was a giant hoof about three inches from my face as I lay with my head between the hooves of the cow I had been working on. The next old cow that had caused all the trouble had reared up on top of the roan cow and was pushing, fighting and hollering fit to be tied. She was really mad about something. Ten other cows, not to be left out had pushed their way down the alley and were lunging with all their strength trying to go ahead. I had serious problems and remember thinking how good it was I had participated in the schnapps bottle and how lucky I was to have made such a great new friend in Bob.

Once you get that many cows pushing down an alley it is almost impossible to make them back up. The cowboys were at a loss as to how to get me out of there. The walls were solid so I couldn't roll out. I couldn't go ahead under the cow because of the gate on the front and going backwards was out of the question. It dawned on me I was in quite a spot and would be lucky to come of this deal without some serious injuries. I could hear the guys talking it over and it wasn't much help to my state of mind. They didn't have a clue.

After several minutes of brainstorming the boss took the bull by the horns and made a decision.

"Open the gate, boys! We'll just have to let these cows out and rescue the poor devil."

The problem was, ten cows would have to go over the top of me to get out. I could feel the broken ribs, arms and legs already. The next thing I knew cattle were exploding over me out the gate. Hooves were everywhere. I made what seemed to be some very acute observations about bovine anatomy as each cow went by. Every cow has at least eight very large hooves. They all have heads as big as a bushel basket and their breath smells like peppermint schnapps mixed with stale silage. As each hoof made a near miss or a direct hit on my exposed backside I remember thinking, "Next time I should bring my own drinks so my new friend Bob won't get to thinking I'm some kind of moocher."

As I crawled out the end of the alley, I was in a state of euphoria. A close call but no broken bones. Some black and blue spots, but chances were I was going to live and I knew Bob had at least two good swallows left in the schnapps bottle.

Harold and Bob were standing at the end of the alley looking like a pair of humbled cowhands. They expected at least a good tongue lashing but that was far from my mind I was just glad to see my two new friends.

I told them so, "Haroold, Bobby," I slurred "I's ser good to see you guys. I ser appreate your showin me how to preg tes cos this fas."

I always pass on the schnapps bottle after that day at the Forsythe ranch. Unless of course it's after 5 p.m.

Humane Isn't Always Black And White

The call came from the county sheriff about ten a.m. on a hot summer day. I didn't like the sound of it. Abuse cases are never easy and they seldom make you new friends.

"Doc, we need you to help us over in Brandon to get rid of some dogs that are being neglected. Think you could help us for an hour or two this afternoon?"

Brandon was a small settlement no longer in the category of being called a town. It consisted of twenty homes, no businesses, and maybe thirty nondescript citizens of varying ages and occupations. The group had a rather unsavory reputation among the local gentry, especially the law enforcement people and county officials. I seldom entered the area mostly due to a lack of purpose but occasionally a dog or cat would cross my table from this little slum on the prairie. All the animals from Brandon had one thing in common: they all had fleas, bad fleas. The sheriff gave me more bad news.

"Some people from the humane society are coming in and we have a court order to search a house up there and euthanise some dogs if we determine they are being abused. We need a vet to put them to sleep."

I wasn't sure what the proper response would be. I didn't want anything to do with this mess, so in my usual forceful way I tried to get out of it.

"I suppose I can help if you really need me but I'd rather not. Can't the humane people do this? I thought that was their job."

"I guess it is but the judge says we need a vet to determine if they have been abused and do the actual euthanasia."

I couldn't believe my eyes, it looked like a scene from Star Wars as I drove up to the little ramshackle house that had been described to me. Standing around were the sheriff, two deputies, and three women from the humane society, all dressed in some type of white protective clothing with face masks, plastic boots, and gloves. My greeting to the sheriff was somewhat of a classic, "Hey Tom, did the little green men land with their dogs or what?"

"You won't think it's so funny when you get inside. This is the worse mess I ever saw."

One of the ladies from the humane society, apparently the leader, immediately tried to pick a fight for some reason. I think she had a

chip on her shoulder from being overly self-righteous for too long.

"We don't see anything hilarious about poor neglected animals. Have you ever investigated an animal abuse case before?"

I was properly chagrined.

The lady's name I found out was Hilary and she was obviously taking her job very seriously. She was a large woman who was used to having her own way and would overpower anyone with the audacity to doubt a single one of her proclamations. She had piercing blue eyes that would bore right through you and make you feel like an absolute moron if you were asinine enough to question her authority. I had worked with humane people before on a limited basis and had always found them to be dedicated sincere people with the world's worst job but Hilary and I probably wouldn't end up lifelong friends. She made me feel like someone was rubbing a dried out sunflower stalk on my back.

The sheriff continued, "We can't catch the dogs so would like you to go in with us and make your determination. Then we'll use our snares and bring them out. Here is your protective clothing. You'll need it to go inside."

Now I really felt like an idiot, but these people were supposed to know what they were doing so maybe I better heed their warning. I still had a little concern however.

"What about the owner? What if he comes home while we're in there?"

Hilary straightened me out, "They took off like a bunch of scared rabbits when we got here and served the warrant. We've been after these people for a long time and now we finally got them."

"How do you know they are not taking care of their dogs. Have you seen them do anything?"

"We know because the neighbors turned in a complaint and they wouldn't let us in the house without a search warrant. If they didn't have something to hide, they would have let us in weeks ago. I've been here four times trying to see these dogs and it's a sixty-mile drive one way. These people have treated me like I was the Gestapo or something."

As I entered the house, I realized Tom was right. The junk was overwhelming: stacked to the ceiling were garbage, papers, old cans, and every other item under the sun littering every square inch. A tiny path made its way through the maze into the kitchen and up the stairs. The most terrible smell imaginable permeated the entire home. I was glad to have my protective clothing on. This was the only place I've ever been in that would compare to a hog finishing barn for odor. Even with the white space suit I could tell the fetor was creeping into my clothes and the pores of my skin. I just wanted to get the heck out of this nightmare as quickly as possible. We soon found the dogs in an upstairs bedroom under an unbelievably dirty old wire springs and mattress.

The pack consisted of a mother and four half-grown puppies of undetermined origin. They looked a lot like rat terriers but were pure white with the unmistakable jutting lower jaws and maligned teeth that spoke of inbreeding. They looked scared but seemed to be in good health and quite happy with their home.

Hilary with her trusty snare jumped into action. She pushed her way in front of me and tried to lay a noose around the first puppy. In 1.5 seconds the dogs were long gone among the various piles of junk, they had their own little tunnels and knew every square inch of their home. Catching these guys with a snare was not going to be easy.

After several more futile minutes of searching, the entire posse held a seminar on the front lawn to plan their next attack. Hilary informed us of the plan.

"We'll stay here all night if necessary but I will catch these poor animals and do something with them. This is outrageous."

My plan was a little simpler.

"You guys stay outside and I'll see if I can talk them in. They only seem scared and may be happy to come to a kind word. Let me try it."

It worked like a charm. I sat down on the floor in a relatively open area and started gently talking to the little guys. Within a minute or two, little heads started poking out of the piles and within ten minutes I had three pups eating some dog biscuits I had in my pocket. They were really quite nice little guys.

As I carried the four puppies outside, it started to dawn on me that I might not be doing the right thing. After doing a physical on the dogs, I discovered a ton of fleas and a possible case of mange but no major problems. The dogs seemed well-fed, clean and healthy.

I tried to break the news to Hilary as gently as I could.

"I noticed a dish of dog food by the door in the kitchen and a bowl of water. It looks like they've been taking care of the dogs as good as a lot of people do."

That wasn't the kind of conclusion she wanted me to draw. In fact she wasn't about to sit still for any such nonsense.

"Can't you smell that odor in the house and can't you see the fleas on these poor little things? You haven't had any experience with neglected animals before have you?"

I started to boil a little inside.

"If I euthanised every farm dog that had fleas and lived in a smelly barn, I'd soon kill ninety per cent of the dogs in the county. Why don't we just cool it here today and I'll talk to the owners and treat the dogs for fleas and mange? Then everyone can have what they want."

She never heard a word I said.

"It just so happens I know a veterinarian back in the city who knows what he's doing. I'll take these poor little things back with me and have him put them down."

I turned to the sheriff for some support.

"Do you really think this is necessary, Tom? I just can't see killing someone's dogs just because I don't agree with their lifestyle. What do you think?"

"You might be right, Doc but I'm required by law to do what she wants so I guess my hands are tied."

I could see I was fighting a losing battle so I did the only thing I could think of on such short notice. I scooped all four of the puppies up and carried them quickly back into the house. Turning them loose in the piles of debris I stomped my feet and hollered as loud as I could at the frightened little dogs. They vanished like four little white ghosts. At least I felt a little better.

Hillary was fit to be tied but I was taking no prisoners by this time.

"I demand you catch those dogs and bring them right back out here. How dare you interfere with a judge's order?"

"I caught the dogs and I turned them loose again. Now you can catch your own victims. I want nothing to do with this lynching."

I tossed and turned all night, reliving the situation, trying to find a better solution, trying to do more to save the little family from an ego too big for such an important job. I never had much luck.

The next morning about 7:30 Tom called to fill me in.

"You'll be happy to hear she never did catch those dogs, Doc. We were there until ten and they finally gave up trying to snare them in the dark. What a mess."

"Do you think she'll give up now or will she come back?"

"I just talked to the judge and got him to rescind the warrant so I think it's all over for now anyway."

I felt like a 100 pound weight had been lifted from my shoulders. Another 100 pounds were added about nine o'clock though when the dog's owner showed up at the clinic.

I had never seen him before but he looked a lot like his house and smelled just as bad. The odor permeated the waiting room in about three seconds.

The little man stood about four foot eleven, weighed about 90 pounds and had weeping, sad eyes that could have come from a basset. His clothes were as dirty as his house and the ground-in dirt on his face and hair was beyond imagination. I knew who it was by the smell – it had a way of being recognized.

He didn't mince words, as he looked me in the eye "I saw you in my house yesterday with those people. What were you doing?"

My self-esteem shrunk to the size of a green snap pea. This was the hardest question I had ever been asked in my life. What was I doing there?

"I guess the humane people don't think you're taking good care of the dogs. They wanted me to kill them but I refused. Maybe you'll have to start looking after them a little better from now on."

For a long minute he just stood there looking at me. Then without warning a larger than life tear slowly rolled down his cheek leaving a trail as it made its way through the dirt and grime. This was followed by the most innocent statement I've ever had the misfortune to hear.

"But..but they're all I have. You can't hurt my friends."

Visions of dead dogs and what could have been went through my head. What if I would have buckled under to Hillary's dominance? My day became bright and beautiful. The 100 pound weight slid off my back. I smiled and led the little man out the door as his tears flowed freely now.

"You wait out here and I'll get some medicine for the fleas and mange. Then we'll talk a little about how to take better care of things. Anyone that tries to take your friends will have to deal with me. Don't you worry."

Pulling Calves Can Be Easy

Herman was one of those hyperexcitable people who can make you nervous just being around them. He was a little, short guy weighing about 150 pounds when soaking wet, with darting eyes, quick motions and a mouth that never quit. He had a very annoying habit of always interrupting you just when you were about to tell him what was wrong with his animal. A conversation might go something like this.

"What do you think is wrong, Doc? She's been straining for two days now and nothing seems to happen. Calf must be breeched. I'm sure it's dead."

"Let me check her and..

"No use spending any money on it. She'll probably die anyway."

My comments get more lengthy as I feel inside the heifer.

"It feels like she isn't.."

"I know it isn't alive 'cause John had one like this a few years back and the calf was dead before we even started."

"Could be, but this one is.."

"Do you think we could butcher her? It wouldn't be a complete loss then."

"I'm sure we can ..."

"What do you think, Doc.? Maybe we should just let nature take its course. Sure would hate to send good money after bad."

"I think we should..."

"Have you ever seen one like this before? You're not going to charge me for a dead calf are you? And the heifer will probably die too. These kind always do."

"I'd like to..."

"Do you think we should give her some penicillin? I don't think it will do any good but at least we can say we tried."

123

"The truth of the matter is ..."

"This has just been a really bad year. Seems like nothing goes right, and now this. What do you think we should do, Doc.?"

"It's really quite simple, we can just ...."

"I suppose we could cut the calf out her side but the last one I had never did breed back so that doesn't work either. Have you been doing a lot of these kind this spring?"

Needless to say communicating with Herman was a challenge.

Herman always calved out a big bunch of heifers and the truth was he was extremely unhandy when it came to delivering calves. In fact he was terrible. He had developed a unique method of covering himself though.

Whenever he had a heifer in trouble or thought he did, he would get everything ready to pull the calf then just before he started he would have his wife call us. Every call was the same, "We have to have a vet right now. We have a heifer in trouble and the calf will be dead if you don't come right away. You better hurry!

With this message out, Herman figured he could start working on the heifer and if he got into real trouble the vet would be along any minute to help him out. You see he lived twenty-four miles from town so he knew he had at least a half-hour to fool around. The wife would stand by ready to race to the house and call us back if he did manage to get the calf out. Our problem was that at some point in time we had let Herman get away with not paying for a trip charge if we didn't actually pull on the yard, so if we were even a mile away and he could get word to our office that he didn't need us he would refuse to pay for the trip. Herman could be a real stinker.

I remember one time in particular when we actually made it on the yard and up to the barn. As I stepped out of my truck, the noise from

inside sounded like financial ruin was eminent. The wife was screaming and Herman was screaming right back.

"Hurry up, they'll be here any minute."

"The stupid puller keeps slipping. I told you we needed a new puller, I'll have him in a minute. You head for the phone. Hurry!"

I almost collided with the miss'ess, as Herman called her, when I opened the barn door to see what was happening. Both faces fell as if disaster had struck. They would have to pay for my call. But all was not lost. Perhaps they could still avoid the actual charge for pulling the calf.

Herman screamed, "Close the door! Can't you see she could get away. Just wait a minute, Doc. I've got her out. We won't need you after all."

With that the wife slammed the door in my face and locked the inside latch, no sense in taking any chances. A few more minutes of commotion from inside and then all was quiet. The pair slowly opened the door both looking a little sheepish. Had they gone too far? What could I say?

"Did you get him out alive?"

A look of relief crossed their faces. Doc wasn't going to be mad.

"You bet," was Herman's now confident response, "It takes a tough one to stump me. You're not going to charge for the trip, are you? After all you didn't actually do anything."

Herman could be very trying at times.

Probably my most memorable calf call with Herman came one late spring day when the miss'ess called with the usual urgency,

"Can you really hurry? We have an emergency! The calf is just too big and won't come. He's still alive so get here as fast as you can. Herman is with her (big surprise). They're out north of the trees in the pasture. You can turn in the gate on the corner. You better hurry!"

By this time we had a policy of waiting for at least a half hour before starting out, just in case so to speak, but it just happened I was only a few miles away when the call came on my radio. Within four minutes Keith and I pulled up to the gate.

Keith realized what was happening quicker than I did.

"My God, do you see what that idiot is doing?" was his first remark.

"I don't believe it! No way! What's he thinking of? Let's get over there." I was a little shook, this could be a wreck.

Herman was one of those guys who loved his four wheeler and felt you could do anything with this versatile little vehicle, including pull calves. Four wheelers are small all terrain vehicles that will go almost anywhere and are very useful around the farm. They are about the size of two motorcycles hooked together, have four-wheel drive and are tough as nails. Great for checking cows, riding fences and numerous other chores, not so great when used as calf pullers.

It was easy to see what had happened. The old cow was so busy with birthing she hadn't noticed Herman drive up behind her on his little machine. Herman, being the alert individual he was, had realized he could sneak up behind the down cow and tie a rope to the calf's legs, nothing wrong with that. Now comes the tricky part though — as soon as you start to pull on the calf, the cow usually realizes something is up and gets to her feet. Being a typical cow, she now heads for parts unknown taking whatever is hooked to her along. His dumb idea might have actually worked if he would have hooked the rope to the four wheeler and gave it a gentle tug but for some strange reason, Herman had decided he shouldn't risk his precious machine and had tied the rope around his waist.

That was the sight we were commenting on as we drove through the gate. Herman was sitting on his four wheeler, tied to the cow and slowly driving ahead taking the slack out of the thirty-foot lariat rope. We were still about a hundred yards away when the rope became tight.

I'll never forget the look on that old cow's face as she felt the pull and set up to look over her shoulder at these strange happenings. She never lost any time! Herman shot off that seat like he was catapulted. The cow gained momentum with every step as she felt the strange anchor pulling on her. The four wheeler kept right on going, headed for the neighbor's stock dam where it eventually came to rest after taking out three fences. We gunned our truck as I prepared my rope hoping to save poor old Herman before this whole situation got out of hand.

Keith, to his credit, was the first one to see the humor in the whole thing. "Say Doc, you suppose Herman will let us charge him for the trip this time?"

My answer was a real gem. "Maybe we should wait and see if he gets the calf pulled before we interfere. After all he does seem to have things under control."

By this time that old cow really had up a head of steam. Herman was only hitting the ground about every ten feet or so. We were rapidly closing on the scene and the four wheeler was ripping through its first fence. That's when things got out of hand.

As we caught up to Herman, I had what seemed like a good idea at the time. I would jump out and grab the rope between the two, surely I could hold that cow with Herman's weight helping me. I hadn't figured on two things: the cow's power and Herman's death grip once he got fastened onto my legs. Suddenly, I was part of the train. Fortunately my weight had slowed the cow down about ten percent or so. Unfortunately she chose this time to head for the hayrack. There were several things around the hayrack. The most obvious being a lot of very wet, very deep and very smelly mud and manure, and the most dangerous being a lot of other cows who hadn't seemed much interested in this whole procedure up to now. Our cow had obviously decided the safest place to be with these idiots dragging along behind was in with the herd.

Panic among the cows: suddenly underfoot were two humans. All I could see were hooves and crap flying as everyone tried at one time to make an exit. It seemed like every cow in the herd just had to exit between our cow and Herman. Every cow seemed to get her legs tangled up in the rope as she fled. Herman was a tough little bugger. He hung on to my legs like we were tied together. I guess he figured if he had to pay me while getting himself killed, he would darn well make sure I went down with him.

Suddenly our luck changed: out slipped the calf - free at last! Suddenly our luck changed back: that old cow was very protective and loved her new little calf more than life it-self. I had already freed myself from Herman so I quickly saved myself by jump-ing up on the hayrack. He was still tied to the calf, not a good thing. The few square inches of Herman that wasn't covered with manure were soon taken care of as that old cow rolled him around in the slop. Af-ter several rolls she made a mistake. She shoved him under the hayrack and out of reach.

I've always thought Herman's first remark was a classic as he poked his head out from under the rack and looked up at me.

"Say Doc. I did half the work pulling that bugger so it seems to me like you should only charge half price. What do you think?"

Everything Is As Bad As It Can Get And Getting Worse

With one quick, unhesitating motion I opened the skin for about 14 inches. A few quick swipes through the muscle, then scissor work until suddenly the air rushed into the large Holstein cow. This was always the scary part. What if she laid down about now and lost her intestine out on the barn floor? What if the halter broke and she took off through the door and out into the pasture with a one-foot incision in her side? But you can't be worried all the time. It hardly ever happened and I just had to see what the heck was going on inside this old cow.

It had all started two days before with a call from John. John was one of my more fastidious clients. He always thought everything just  had to have a perfect solution with no mess and no fuss. The minute anything started to go the least bit out of the ordinary, John would immediately abandon ship on me. He just knew it was no use to bother treating a sick animal – it was going to die anyway. Clients like John would keep you on your toes at least: syringe getting dirty? He'd soon tell you about it. Arrive with your coveralls a little smeared up? He'd let you know he didn't appreciate it one bit. I liked John a lot. This particular call had seemed a little out of the ordinary for John. He had seemed quite upset which wasn't his way at all.

"Can you come out this morning, Doc? I have my best Holstein off-feed and looking poorly. She'll probably die anyway but at least we could give it a try," John opened, and followed with, "Sure hate to lose her. She's worth at least $1500."

I opened with my best salvo, "It's probably nothing too serious John. Maybe she just ate something that didn't agree with her. I'll check her out right away. She'll probably be OK."

129

"Well, all right, but I'm probably just sending good money after bad."

The first time I ran into John's attitude was several years ago when I had been called to look at a horse he was keeping for his granddaughter. The old gelding had long ago past twenty years on the time chart and was sadly looking his age. The old  timer was spitting out his oats and looking thin as a rail. John himself thought it was crazy to even think of working on the old guy but a fifteen-year old granddaughter is hard to deny no matter how pessimistic you strive to be. The diagnosis was easy, even without an exam you could tell he was in bad need of some minor dental work.

"No problem," I told the pair, "We can just float his teeth a minute and take off the spurs. He will be as good as new in a few days."

After I explained to them the reason for the problem and the solution, John had an immediate response.

"You mean to tell me a horse's teeth just keep growing out for twenty or even thirty years and have to wear themselves off? I never heard of anything so crazy. Whoever designed that system must have been a little fuzzy in the head."

Then I showed him an equine dental float and explained what I was going to do.

"Doc, you're crazy. There's no way you can file down a horse's teeth with that contraption without getting your fool head kicked off."

"John," I said, "just relax. I've done this a hundred times and it just about always works out great."

He wasn't convinced.

"I think we'll just save our money and put him down. I can use the twelve gauge and take him out of his misery in a second. These kind of things never work anyway and sooner or later you end up doing away with him."

The granddaughter now jumped into the fray and ended it in a hurry.

"Grampa, just shut up and get ready to pay the man. We're not going to shoot Sparky so just get that idea out of your head right now."

John did as he was told and Sparky got along just fine for two more years until one cold winter he expired during the night from a bad case of old age.

As I drove out to John's this morning to check the sick cow, I remembered another incident and chuckled to myself. It had been two years ago in the spring when we were castrating a few beef calves out at his place. One of the calves had ruptured during the procedure and his intestines had come out of the incision to the outside. It looked appalling. John, having never seen anything so ghastly in his life, panicked.

"Hold him down," he shouted. "I'll get the gun and put him out of his misery." With that he raced to the house for his faithful twelve gauge.

"No!" I cried, "He'll be OK. This happens quite often. I can fix it in a minute."

Quickly I grabbed my suture and needle, pushed all the parts back where they belonged and closed up the tear. It all took about five minutes. By the time John came back with his trusty cannon, the calf was out with the bunch quietly sucking his mother no worse for his near death experience.

"Don't shoot! You'll hit the cow," was the friendly advice one of the cowboys threw at him.

Another said, "Be careful, John. You'll blow your foot off."

And of course I had to get my two-cents worth in, "Be sure to shoot him in the head so you make a clean kill."

"You guys laugh all you want. He'll never make it," John remarked balefully.

All summer long, every time I saw John in town or happened to be out at his place, I just had to rib him a little about the calf, but his answer was always the same, "He ain't out of the woods yet. Something like that always kills a calf sooner or later."

Six months later as I got out of my truck at John's place to vaccinate some calves; I noticed he had a rather smug look on his face. As we walked to the barn, I found out why.

"I sure wish you would have let me shoot that bad calf last spring like I wanted to. Turns out I just fed the cow all summer for nothing. He's dead you know."

My mouth fell open in surprise, "What the heck happened? He's been doing good all summer."

"Last Sunday morning I found him all bloated up out by the feed bunk, died before chore time."

"But, John," I asked, "Why in the world didn't you call me? We probably could have saved him."

"No use, I knew he was going to die, just like I said."

What more can you say?

So here I was getting ready to do battle with the world's worst pessimist one more time as I drove on his yard. It started as soon as I stepped out of the truck.

"Maybe you just as well go back to town, Doc. It sure looks bad to me."

"Well, let's take a look before we do anything rash. What do you say?"

The big old Holstein didn't give me much to go on: temperature up a little, listless, eyes sunk a little. Sick but nothing you could really put your finger on. To put it another way, I didn't have a clue. After drawing some blood and collecting some urine, I gave John my favorite line of bull when I wasn't sure what was going on.

"I'll have to do some lab work on her before I can say anything for sure, John, but don't you worry now. We'll get to the bottom of this."

"She'll probably be dead by morning, Doc. Better not come out unless I call you."

"John, she won't be dead. We have to be positive about these things, OK?"

The lab work didn't help a bit. I was at a loss but was pretty sure the whole problem evolved around her intestines. By the next morning it was obvious that she was going down hill. Something had to be done.

So I found myself with a 14 inch incision in the flank of a 1500 pound cow hoping something good would come out of this whole mess. It didn't. The first thing I saw as I pulled up a loop of small intestine was a massive infection. Peritonitis, the infection was already advanced to the terminal stages where the intestines were growing together and if not completely closed they had to be very close. This cow was a goner.

"I'm afraid you're right this time John. Nothing I can do for this poor old girl." I remarked as I showed him the lesions and explained what they meant.

"Well, at least we tried, but I knew she was going to die. These kind always do, you know."

I didn't see John again all that summer and had pretty well forgotten the whole unfortunate episode until that fall when I once again pulled on the yard to vaccinate some calves.

The first words out of his mouth made my day.

"You were right about that cow, Doc."

"Yeah, too bad, that's one time I'd like to have been wrong. How long did the old girl last?"

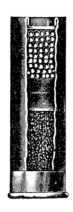

"That was the strange part about the whole thing. I turned her out to the creek pasture to let her die but she just didn't seem to want to get the job done. She even started eating a little grass and put on some weight this fall."

"You mean to tell me she was still alive this fall. Why in the world didn't you call me and let me have another look? I must have been wrong about how bad she was. Maybe we could have saved her yet with a little treatment."

"It didn't matter, Doc. Those kind always die anyway. No sense in sending good money after bad."

"Yeah but, all we would've had to do was get her good enough to sell, she might have brought you five or six hundred dollars. How did she look when she died anyway?"

"She looked great but you said she was going to die and I just got sick and tired of waiting for her so I took the old 12-gauge and put her out of her misery."

Spring Is No Time For Sleep

My day started at seven, with nothing too exciting going on. The spring calving was just starting so one vet could still handle the night calls easily and the other could sleep all night. We knew Mother Nature was waiting like a loaded gun ready to break out any day now. So well-rested and full of good cheer I started the day with a routine prolapse, a sick milk cow, a few sick calves, a horse with some strange scabs on his neck, and two dogs to vaccinate for rabies. Perhaps enough work to keep me busy until eleven or so. My partner, Dr. Holt, who had been out twice during the night was sleeping in late and wouldn't make an appearance until eight o'clock. Around 7:45 spring hit with a vengeance. My secretary popped on the radio with some news.

"Can you swing over to the Peterson's? They have a heifer that needs a Caesarian right away. Also, John Swimmer has a uterine prolapse that needs attention as soon as possible."

Great, she just added another two hours worth of work onto my morning and an additional sixty miles of driving. Five minutes later she came back on.

"More good news, the Johnson ranch has a heifer calving and will need some help. Sounds like another Caesarian. They seem quite anxious."

"Do I have a partner in this business or what?" was my sarcastic answer.

"Yes," she said, "And I have him out on two other calving calls and a prolapse south of town. When you get done, maybe you can help him finish up!"

This was the early 1970s, when the so called "exotic cattle" were first introduced onto the Great Plains, to improve our genetics and help us sell more pounds of beef in the fall. Unfortunately the cattle we had been raising for the last sixty years were much smaller and could not handle the larger calves produced with the superior genetics. Many of the crossbred calves had to come out the side. They were just too big. It made for some interesting springs as this day was attesting to.

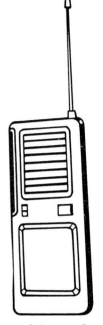

By the middle of the afternoon I was starting on the routine calls that had been lined up that morning and hoping things might settle down a little before evening. This day was meant to be a tough one. The calving calls just kept coming until 10 p.m. when, lo and behold, I found myself caught up. Dr. Holt had been home for an hour or so already. It was his night off.

That pillow felt so good I couldn't believe it, probably because I only got to feel it for about two minutes when the phone rang. I managed to get my boots on and start out the door before it rang again, and the third time I heard my wife answer it just as I was getting into my truck. A uterine prolapse and two Caesarians staring at me just like that plus about fifty miles of driving.

At one a.m. I was once again finished and home. My head hit the pillow like a pumpkin dropped from a haymow. It lasted for four minutes when that black nightmare rang again. I hate it when the conversation starts out, "Are you awake, Doc?" This time it was Dave Ellis, who was our most far flung client to the northwest.

"I have a heifer calving, Doc. Looks like a Caesarian to me. How soon can you get here?"

Just as I was pulling onto the yard at Dave's my wife came on the radio, "Can you go down to the Johnson's again? They have another heifer calving and need you right away."

"Holy cow, I'm 75 miles from their place. You better call Dr. Holt and talk him into going."

I hate it when she sounds so cheerful delivering bad news.

"Sorry, I already sent him southwest of town on two other calving calls so you should get there faster than him."

Five o'clock and I'm finished. Whoops, my wife is on the radio again. The morning calls have started. One more uterine prolapse by 7 a.m. and I've got twenty-four hours under my belt. The good news is Keith will be driving for me today so I should get some sleep on the road. After a few springs it's amazing how you adapt to sleeping between calls, during meals, and on piles of hay when you catch a spare minute on a farm. This particular day, Dr. Holt and I happened to hit town at noon and shared lunch. The talk, as always, evolved around hiring another veterinarian. Did we have enough work? How would we pay his wages? etc. Thirty minutes later, we are back on the road. He goes west and I go north into a steady stream of calving, lambing, prolapses, calf scours, pneumonia, and other emergencies. This time of year we don't have time for regular work. If it isn't an emergency, it will have to wait for another day.

By 9 p.m. I'm home again and once more my head hits the pillow like a wet sack of sand dropped from the water tower. Too tired to sleep I toss and turn for a few minutes until the black monster rings its shrill warning. It's not fair! I'm not on call! Please let it be for my wife. It's not. It's Dr. Holt's wife needing help. He's hopelessly behind and could I run down to Bill Green's and do a quick Caesarian? Pulling on my pants and still warm boots I have a great idea: I'll take my wife along to drive. I must have been a little punchy to ever dream up an idea this hair-brained. Would you want to share a late night experience with your spouse if that person hadn't had any real sleep for 39 hours?

Things were going rather well until we got out of the driveway and she made her first big mistake of the evening, she spoke.

"You'll have to tell me where we're going. I don't have the slightest idea."

Her speaking wasn't the worst part, what caused all the trouble was her happy, friendly voice. It grated like someone had rubbed my bare back with a frayed cable from a worn out calf puller. My answer was, I thought, quite inspired.

"Why are you along if you don't even know where the Greens live, for crying out loud?"

"A little snippy, are we? Maybe I won't be along much longer if you can't act a little civilized. In fact maybe I should turn around right

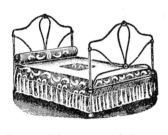

now and go back to bed were I belong. What do you think of that big boy?"

Fortunately for me I knew she was just kidding and besides she had the good sense to not give me any more of her happy late night chitchat as we drove the twenty miles out to the farm. This group of Greens were almost unknown to me and I had no idea what to expect as we pulled up to the barn. The wife was standing waiting for us by the door.

"Bill isn't here He had a meeting in town tonight and I'm afraid I'm not much help. I'm sure glad you brought an assistant along."

I looked her in the eye and didn't have the slightest idea what she was talking about. In fact I wasn't even sure why I was here. My wife tried to help me out and proceeded to get her head bit off by my happy-go-lucky charm.

"Do you want me to help you get your stuff together?" was her innocent question.

"Did you come to help or watch? Of course I need all the help I can get. Can't you see that?"

Her answer was something about the help I was going to need if something didn't change but I didn't catch it all and soon forgot to seek further enlightenment as we carried my equipment into the barn and saw the nightmare waiting for us.

The heifer was in a box stall about fifteen-feet square without a post or any holes in the side to tie a rope through. The rest of the barn was one big open area much too large to try and handle a worked-up heifer. Not only that but the area was full of used farm machinery so letting her out of the stall was not an option. I asked the obvious question: "Do you have someplace we can catch her?"

Mrs. Green had a quick tongue, "You're the vet. You're supposed to know how to do things like that. I never mess with this stuff."

Still stymied, I explored another angle, "When do you expect your husband to get home? Maybe he would have an idea."

"He'll show up when the bar closes I'm sure. If he was home where he belongs, we wouldn't need you now, would we? He can pull any calf that comes along and doesn't need to waste money on a vet except when he's out snortin' at the pool hall."

My lack of sleep caught up to me. I opened the sliding door on the stall and slipped inside to look things over. The heifer responded in a second. Her eyeballs enlarged to the size of pie plates and her ears jerked up like they had been pulled with a sky hook. I jumped, grabbed a rafter and pulled up just as her head crashed into the wall where I had been standing. She came unglued, and I was stuck up in the rafters over her head with no way out and no way to catch her. All I could think about was a nice warm bed and a cup of cocoa. My wife not realizing this wasn't the normal way of doing things, urged me on.

"Can you hurry it up a little? I'm getting cold standing around waiting for you."

Seeing a hole in the box wall up in the rafters, I had an idea that just might work. If I could get my rope up here, I could slip a noose on the critter, tie it to a rafter and pull her up snug. Great idea! Slipping

my hand out the six-inch hole, I gently asked Mrs. Green to hand me the rope.

"Why don't you get down from there and come out here and get it yourself?"

"Because that heifer is mad at me for some reason and I don't care to be flattened like a pancake. Would you just hand me the rope?"

She muttered to herself as she slipped the end of the rope through the hole. "If my husband was here he, wouldn't let one little heifer scare the bejejus out of him."

It was a simple matter to rope the heifer. I just dropped the loop straight down and had her. The fun started when she felt it tighten around her neck. She went nuts. Even with the rope wrapped tight as I could get it, she still had enough slack to go round and round down below me, fighting like a tied up wild cat. She really got mad at me now. My forty or so hours without sleep did wonders for my sense of humor as the whole situation turned funny and I started to laugh. In fact I became almost hysterical. This had to be the funniest thing I had ever seen. Here was this crazy veterinarian with no real plan trying to pull a calf out of a heifer he couldn't get close to far less work on, while being stuck in the rafters with no way down and no idea what to do if he could get down. My laughter was infectious and soon the two women were joining in the fun with as much gusto as me.

"Maybe you should put salt on her tail. I've heard that always works," my wife chortled, "Or perhaps you could whisper in her ear. You're so good at it."

Not to be undone, her companion had a hint or two for me, "Why don't you poke her with a stick? That always gets their attention. Or better yet why not grab her ear and make her know who's boss?" She could hardly spit it out she was laughing so hard.

I suddenly had a great idea. If I had my other rope, I could win this stand off. Tying the first rope, I had them pass me the second one and proceeded to put my plan into action. Very carefully I dangled the loop down until I had it under and around her tail, next I pulled her tail straight up until the rope tightened around the switch and held firm, I had her. A cow's tail is tougher than nails. In fact she can pull a one bottom plow with it, if the rope's tied on properly, and not seem to feel a thing. She was now tied on both ends and best of all couldn't fall down while I worked on her.

Just as I started my examination who should walk in the door but Bill, home from the meeting and pool hall, full of good cheer. As he looked at my apparatus, I could tell he was very impressed, so naturally I acted like this was a common procedure for handling unruly cows.

"Yep," I said, "I had to use the old rafter trick on this one. She was trying to get me and it called for some fast work."

The women were beside themselves, but they played along laughing all the time. As I delivered a struggling little black bull calf, the good will and fellowship continued to strengthen among us, even the heifer seemed to settle down as we laughed and joked. It was eleven when we finally pulled off the yard and suddenly my entire body seemed to collapse. I just couldn't hold my head up one more minute.

As I drifted into sleep, my wife's words flowed over me like a warm blanket. "I never realized how much fun you have at work. You're really lucky, you know."

And so another spring began.

Since you have enjoyed this book, perhaps you would be interested in some of these others from QUIXOTE PRESS.

ARKANSAS BOOKS

HOW TO TALK ARKANSAS
    by Bruce Carlson .... paperback $7.95
ARKANSAS' ROADKILL COOKBOOK
    by Bruce Carlson .... paperback $7.95
REVENGE OF ROADKILL
    by Bruce Carlson .... paperback $7.95
GHOSTS OF THE OZARKS
    by Bruce Carlson .... paperback $9.95
A FIELD GUIDE TO SMALL ARKANSAS FEMALES
    by Bruce Carlson .... paperback $9.95
LET'S US GO DOWN TO THE RIVER 'N...
    by various authors .... paperback $9.95
ARKANSAS' VANISHING OUTHOUSE
    by Bruce Carlson .... paperback $9.95
TALL TALES OF THE MISSISSIPPI RIVER
    by Dan Titus .... paperback $9.95
LOST & BURIED TREASURE OF THE MISSISSIPPI RIVER
    by Netha Bell & Gary Scholl .... paperback $9.95
TALES OF HACKETT'S CREEK
    by Dan Titus .... paperback $9.95
UNSOLVED MYSTERIES OF THE MISSISSIPPI RIVER
    by Netha Bell .... paperback $9.95
101 WAYS TO USE A DEAD RIVER FLY
    by Bruce Carlson .... paperback $7.95
VACANT LOT, SCHOOL YARD & BACK ALLEY GAMES
    by various authors .... paperback $9.95
HOW TO TALK MIDWESTERN
    by Robert Thomas .... paperback $7.95
ARKANSAS COOKIN'
    by Bruce Carlson .... (3x5) paperback $5.95

DAKOTA BOOKS

HOW TO TALK DAKOTA .... paperback $7.95
Some Pretty Tame, but Kinda Funny Stories About Early
DAKOTA LADIES-OF-THE-EVENING
    by Bruce Carlson .... paperback $9.95

SOUTH DAKOTA ROADKILL COOKBOOK
  by Bruce Carlson .... paperback $7.95
REVENGE OF ROADKILL
  by Bruce Carlson .... paperback $7.95
101 WAYS TO USE A DEAD RIVER FLY
  by Bruce Carlson .... paperback $7.95
LET'S US GO DOWN TO THE RIVER 'N...
  by various authors .... paperback $9.95
LOST & BURIED TREASURE OF THE MISSOURI RIVER
  by Netha Bell .... paperback $9.95
MAKIN' DO IN SOUTH DAKOTA
  by various authors .... paperback $9.95
GUNSHOOTIN', WHISKEY DRINKIN', GIRL CHASIN' STORIES
OUT OF THE OLD DAKOTAS
  by Netha Bell .... paperback $9.95
THE DAKOTAS' VANISHING OUTHOUSE
  by Bruce Carlson .... paperback $9.95
VACANT LOT, SCHOOL YARD & BACK ALLEY GAMES
  by various authors .... paperback $9.95
HOW TO TALK MIDWESTERN
  by Robert Thomas .... paperback $7.95
DAKOTA COOKIN'
  by Bruce Carlson .... (3x5) paperback $5.95

ILLINOIS BOOKS

ILLINOIS COOKIN'
  by Bruce Carlson .... (3x5) paperback $5.95
THE VANISHING OUTHOUSE OF ILLINOIS
  by Bruce Carlson .... paperback $9.95
A FIELD GUIDE TO ILLINOIS' CRITTERS
  by Bruce Carlson .... paperback $7.95
YOU KNOW YOU'RE IN ILLINOIS WHEN...
  by Bruce Carlson .... paperback $7.95
Some Pretty Tame, but Kinda Funny Stories About Early
ILLINOIS LADIES-OF-THE-EVENING
  by Bruce Carlson .... paperback $9.95
ILLINOIS' ROADKILL COOKBOOK
  by Bruce Carlson .... paperback $7.95
101 WAYS TO USE A DEAD RIVER FLY
  by Bruce Carlson .... paperback $7.95

HOW TO TALK ILLINOIS
by Netha Bell .... paperback $7.95
TALL TALES OF THE MISSISSIPPI RIVER
by Dan Titus .... paperback $9.95
TALES OF HACKETT'S CREEK
by Dan Titus .... paperback $9.95
UNSOLVED MYSTERIES OF THE MISSISSIPPI
by Netha Bell .... paperback $9.95
LOST & BURIED TREASURE OF THE MISSISSIPPI RIVER
by Netha Bell & Gary Scholl .... paperback $9.95
STRANGE FOLKS ALONG THE MISSISSIPPI
by Pat Wallace .... paperback $9.95
LET'S US GO DOWN TO THE RIVER 'N...
by various authors .... paperback $9.95
MISSISSIPPI RIVER PO' FOLK
by Pat Wallace .... paperback $9.95
GHOSTS OF THE MISSISSIPPI RIVER (from Keokuk to St. Louis)
by Bruce Carlson .... paperback $9.95
GHOSTS OF THE MISSISSIPPI RIVER (from Dubuque to Keokuk)
by Bruce Carlson .... paperback $9.95
MAKIN' DO IN ILLINOIS
by various authors .... paperback $9.95
MY VERY FIRST
by various authors .... paperback $9.95
VACANT LOT, SCHOOL YARD & BACK ALLEY GAMES
by various authors .... paperback $9.95
HOW TO TALK MIDWESTERN
by Robert Thomas .... paperback $7.95

INDIANA BOOKS

HOW TO TALK INDIANA .... paperback $7.95
INDIANA'S ROADKILL COOKBOOK
by Bruce Carlson .... paperback $7.95
REVENGE OF ROADKILL
by Bruce Carlson .... paperback $7.95
A FIELD GUIDE TO SMALL INDIANA FEMALES
by Bruce Carlson .... paperback $9.95
GHOSTS OF THE OHIO RIVER (from Cincinnati to Louisville)
by Bruce Carlson .... paperback $9.95
LET'S US GO DOWN TO THE RIVER 'N...
by various authors .... paperback $9.95

101 WAYS TO USE A DEAD RIVER FLY
    by Bruce Carlson .... paperback $7.95
INDIANA'S VARNISHING OUTHOUSE
    by Bruce Carlson .... paperback $9.95
VACANT LOT, SCHOOL YARD & BACK ALLEY GAMES
    by various authors .... paperback $9.95
HOW TO TALK MIDWESTERN
    by Robert Thomas .... paperback $7.95

IOWA BOOKS

IOWA COOKIN'
    by Bruce Carlson .... (3x5) paperback $5.95
IOWA'S ROADKILL COOKBOOK
    By Bruce Carlson .... paperback $7.95
REVENGE OF ROADKILL
    by Bruce Carlson .... paperback $7.95
IOWA'S OLD SCHOOLHOUSES
    by Carole Turner Johnston .... paperback $9.95
GHOSTS OF THE AMANA COLONIES
    by Lori Erickson .... paperback $9.95
GHOSTS OF THE IOWA GREAT LAKES
    by Bruce Carlson .... paperback $9.95
GHOSTS OF THE MISSISSIPPI RIVER (from Dubuque to Keokuk)
    by Bruce Carlson .... paperback $9.95
GHOSTS OF THE MISSISSIPPI RIVER (from Minneapolis to Dubuque)
    by Bruce Carlson .... paperback $9.95
GHOSTS OF POLK COUNTY, IOWA
    by Tom Welch .... paperback $9.95
TALES OF HACKETT'S CREEK
    by Dan Titus .... paperback $9.95
ME 'N WESLEY (stories about the homemade toys that
    Iowa farm children made and played with around the turn of the century)
    by Bruce Carlson .... paperback $9.95
TALL TALES OF THE MISSISSIPPI RIVER
    by Dan Titus .... paperback $9.95
HOW TO TALK IOWA .... paperback $7.95
UNSOLVED MYSTERIES OF THE MISSISSIPPI
    by Netha Bell .... paperback $9.95
101 WAYS TO USE A DEAD RIVER FLY
    by Bruce Carlson .... paperback $7.95

LET'S US GO DOWN TO THE RIVER 'N...
  by various authors .... paperback $9.95
TRICKS WE PLAYED IN IOWA
  by various authors .... paperback $9.95
IOWA, THE LAND BETWEEN THE VOWELS
  (farm boy stories from the early 1900s)
  by Bruce Carlson .... paperback $9.95
LOST & BURIED TREASURE OF THE MISSISSIPPI RIVER
  by Netha Bell & Gary Scholl .... paperback $9.95
Some Pretty Tame, but Kinda Funny Stories About Early
IOWA LADIES-OF-THE-EVENING
  by Bruce Carlson .... paperback $9.95
THE VANISHING OUTHOUSE OF IOWA
  by Bruce Carlson .... paperback $9.95
IOWA'S EARLY HOME REMEDIES
  by 26 students at Wapello Elem. School .... paperback $9.95
IOWA - A JOURNEY IN A PROMISED LAND
  by Kathy Yoder .... paperback $16.95
LOST & BURIED TREASURE OF THE MISSOURI RIVER
  by Netha Bell .... paperback $9.95
FIELD GUIDE TO IOWA'S CRITTERS
  by Bruce Carlson .... paperback $7.95
OLD IOWA HOUSES, YOUNG LOVES
  by Bruce Carlson .... paperback $9.95
SKUNK RIVER ANTHOLOGY
  by Gene Olson .... paperback $9.95
VACANT LOT, SCHOOL YARD & BACK ALLEY GAMES
  by various authors .... paperback $9.95
HOW TO TALK MIDWESTERN
  by Robert Thomas .... paperback $7.95

KANSAS BOOKS

HOW TO TALK KANSAS .... paperback $7.95
STOPOVER IN KANSAS
  by Jon McAlpin .... paperback $9.95
LET'S US GO DOWN TO THE RIVER 'N ...
  by various authors .... paperback $9.95
LOST & BURIED TREASURE OF THE MISSOURI RIVER
  by Netha Bell .... paperback $9.95

101 WAYS TO USE A DEAD RIVER FLY
 by Bruce Carlson .... paperback $7.95
VACANT LOT, SCHOOL YARD & BACK ALLEY GAMES
 by various authors .... paperback $9.95
HOW TO TALK MIDWESTERN
 by Robert Thomas .... paperback $7.95

KENTUCKY BOOKS

GHOSTS OF THE OHIO RIVER (from Pittsburgh to Cincinnati)
 by Bruce Carlson .... paperback $9.95
GHOSTS OF THE OHIO RIVER (from Cincinnati to Louisville)
 by Bruce Carlson .... paperback $9.95
TALES OF HACKETT'S CREEK
 by Dan Titus .... paperback $9.95
LOST & BURIED TREASURE OF THE MISSISSIPPI RIVER
 by Netha Bell & Gary Scholl .... paperback $9.95
LET'S US GO DOWN TO THE RIVER 'N ...
 by various authors .... paperback $9.95
UNSOLVED MYSTERIES OF THE MISSISSIPPI
 by Netha Bell .... paperback $9.95
101 WAYS TO USE A DEAD RIVER FLY
 by Bruce Carlson .... paperback $7.95
TALL TALES OF THE MISSISSIPPI RIVER
 by Dan Titus .... paperback $9.95
MY VERY FIRST
 by various authors .... paperback $9.95
VACANT LOT, SCHOOL YARD & BACK ALLEY GAMES
 by various authors .... paperback $9.95

MICHIGAN BOOKS

MICHIGAN COOKIN'
 by Bruce Carlson .... (3x5) paperback $5.95
MICHIGAN'S ROADKILL COOKBOOK
 by Bruce Carlson .... paperback $7.95
MICHIGAN'S VANISHING OUTHOUSE
 by Bruce Carlson .... paperback $9.95

MINNESOTA BOOKS

MINNESOTA'S ROADKILL COOKBOOK
    by Bruce Carlson .... paperback $7.95
REVENGE OF ROADKILL
    by Bruce Carlson .... paperback $7.95
A FIELD GUIDE TO SMALL MINNESOTA FEMALES
    by Bruce Carlson .... paperback $9.95
GHOSTS OF THE MISSISSIPPI RIVER (from Minneapolis to Dubuque)
    by Bruce Carlson .... paperback $9.95
LAKES COUNTRY COOKBOOK
    by Bruce Carlson .... paperback $11.95
UNSOLVED MYSTERIES OF THE MISSISSIPPI
    by Netha Bell .... paperback $9.95
TALES OF HACKETT'S CREEK
    by Dan Titus .... paperback $9.95
GHOSTS OF SOUTHWEST MINNESOTA
    by Ruth Hein .... paperback $9.95
HOW TO TALK LIKE A MINNESOTA NATIVE .... paperback $7.95
MINNESOTA'S VANISHING OUTHOUSE
    by Bruce Carlson .... paperback $9.95
TALL TALES OF THE MISSISSIPPI RIVER
    by Dan Titus .... paperback $9.95
Some Pretty Tame, but Kinda Funny Stories About Early
MINNESOTA LADIES-OF-THE-EVENING
    by Bruce Carlson .... paperback $9.95
101 WAYS TO USE A DEAD RIVER FLY .... paperback $7.95
LOST & BURIED TREASURE OF THE MISSISSIPPI RIVER
    by Netha Bell & Gary Scholl .... paperback $9.95
VACANT LOT, SCHOOL YARD & BACK ALLEY GAMES
    by various authors .... paperback $9.95
HOW TO TALK MIDWESTERN
    by Robert Thomas .... paperback $7.95
MINNESOTA COOKIN'
    by Bruce Carlson .... (3x5) paperback $5.95

MISSOURI BOOKS

MISSOURI COOKIN'
    by Bruce Carlson .... (3x5) paperback $5.95
MISSOURI'S ROADKILL COOKBOOK
    by Bruce Carlson .... paperback $7.95

REVENGE OF ROADKILL
    by Bruce Carlson .... paperback $7.95
LET'S US GO DOWN TO THE RIVER 'N ...
    by various authors .... paperback $9.95
LAKES COUNTRY COOKBOOK
    by Bruce Carlson .... paperback $11.95
101 WAYS TO USE A DEAD RIVER FLY
    by Bruce Carlson .... paperback $7.95
TALL TALES OF THE MISSISSIPPI RIVER
    by Dan Titus .... paperback $9.95
TALES OF HACKETT'S CREEK
    by Dan Titus .... paperback $9.95
STRANGE FOLKS ALONG THE MISSISSIPPI
    by Pat Wallace .... paperback $9.95
LOST & BURIED TREASURE OF THE MISSOURI RIVER
    by Netha Bell .... paperback $9.95
HOW TO TALK MISSOURIAN
    by Bruce Carlson .... paperback $7.95
VACANT LOT, SCHOOL YARD & BACK ALLEY GAMES
    by various authors .... paperback $9.95
HOW TO TALK MIDWESTERN
    by Robert Thomas .... paperback $7.95
UNSOLVED MYSTERIES OF THE MISSISSIPPI
    by Netha Bell .... paperback $9.95
LOST & BURIED TREASURE OF THE MISSISSIPPI RIVER
    by Netha Bell & Gary Scholl .... paperback $9.95
MISSISSIPPI RIVER PO' FOLK
    by Pat Wallace .... paperback $9.95
Some Pretty Tame, but Kinda Funny Stories About Early
MISSOURI LADIES-OF-THE-EVENING
    by Bruce Carlson .... paperback $9.95
GUNSHOOTIN', WHISKEY DRINKIN', GIRL CHASIN'
STORIES OUT OF THE OLD MISSOURI TERRITORY
    by Bruce Carlson .... paperback $9.95
THE VANISHING OUTHOUSE OF MISSOURI
    by Bruce Carlson .... paperback $9.95
A FIELD GUIDE TO MISSOURI'S CRITTERS
    by Bruce Carlson .... paperback $7.95
EARLY MISSOURI HOME REMEDIES
    by various authors .... paperback $9.95
GHOSTS OF THE OZARKS
    by Bruce Carlson .... paperback $9.95

MISSISSIPPI RIVER COOKIN' BOOK
        by Bruce Carlson .... paperback $11.95
MISSOURI'S OLD HOUSES, AND NEW LOVES
        by Bruce Carlson .... paperback $9.95
UNDERGROUND MISSOURI
        by Bruce Carlson .... paperback $9.95

NEBRASKA BOOKS

LOST & BURIED TREASURE OF THE MISSOURI RIVER
        by Netha Bell .... paperback $9.95
101 WAYS TO USE A DEAD RIVER FLY
        by Bruce Carlson .... paperback $7.95
LET'S US GO DOWN TO THE RIVER 'N ...
        by various authors .... paperback $9.95
HOW TO TALK MIDWESTERN
        by Robert Thomas .... paperback $7.95
VACANT LOT, SCHOOL YARD & BACK ALLEY GAMES
        by various authors .... paperback $9.95

TENNESSEE BOOKS

TALES OF HACKETT'S CREED
        by Dan Titus .... paperback $9.95
TALL TALES OF THE MISSISSIPPI RIVER
        by Dan Titus .... paperback $9.95
UNSOLVED MYSTERIES OF THE MISSISSIPPI
        by Netha Bell .... paperback $9.95
LOST & BURIED TREASURE OF THE MISSISSIPPI RIVER
        by Netha Bell & Gary Scholl .... paperback $9.95
LET'S US GO DOWN TO THE RIVER 'N ...
        by various authors .... paperback $9.95
101 WAYS TO USE A DEAD RIVER FLY
        by Bruce Carlson .... paperback $7.95
VACANT LOT, SCHOOL YARD & BACK ALLEY GAMES
        by various authors .... paperback $9.95

WISCONSIN BOOKS

HOW TO TALK WISCONSIN .... paperback $7.95
WISCONSIN COOKIN'
     by Bruce Carlson .... (3x5) paperback $5.95
WISCONSIN'S ROADKILL COOKBOOK
     by Bruce Carlson .... paperback $7.95
REVENGE OF ROADKILL
     by Bruce Carlson .... paperback $7.95
TALL TALES OF THE MISSISSIPPI RIVER
     by Dan Titus .... paperback $9.95
LAKES COUNTRY COOKBOOK
     by Bruce Carlson .... paperback $11.95
TALES OF HACKETT'S CREEK
     by Dan Titus .... paperback $9.95
LET'S US GO DOWN TO THE RIVER 'N ...
     by various authors .... paperback $9.95
101 WAYS TO USE A DEAD RIVER FLY
     by Bruce Carlson .... paperback $7.95
UNSOLVED MYSTERIES OF THE MISSISSIPPI
     by Netha Bell .... paperback $9.95
LOST & BURIED TREASURE OF THE MISSISSIPPI RIVER
     by Netha Bell & Gary Scholl .... paperback $9.95
GHOSTS OF THE MISSISSIPPI RIVER (from Dubuque to Keokuk)
     by Bruce Carlson .... paperback $9.95
HOW TO TALK MIDWESTERN
     by Robert Thomas .... paperback $7.95
VACANT LOT, SCHOOL YARD & BACK ALLEY GAMES
     by various authors .... paperback $9.95
MY VERY FIRST
     by various authors .... paperback $9.95
EARLY WISCONSIN HOME REMEDIES
     by various authors .... paperback $9.95
GHOSTS OF THE MISSISSIPPI RIVER (from Minneapolis to Dubuque)
     by Bruce Carlson .... paperback $9.95
THE VANISHING OUTHOUSE OF WISCONSIN
     by Bruce Carlson .... paperback $9.95
GHOSTS OF DOOR COUNTY, WISCONSIN
     by Geri Rider .... paperback $9.95
Some Pretty Tame, but Kinda Funny Stories About Early
WISCONSIN LADIES-OF-THE-EVENING
     by Bruce Carlson .... paperback $9.95

MIDWESTERN BOOKS

A FIELD GUIDE TO THE MIDWEST'S WORST RESTAURANTS
by Bruce Carlson .... paperback $5.95
THE MOTORIST'S FIELD GUIDE TO MIDWESTERN FARM
EQUIPMENT (misguided information as only a city slicker can give it)
by Bruce Carlson .... paperback $5.95
VACANT LOT, SCHOOL YARD & BACK ALLEY GAMES
OF THE MIDWEST YEARS AGO
by various authors .... paperback $9.95
MIDWEST SMALL TOWN COOKING
by Bruce Carlson .... (3x5) paperback $5.95
HITCHHIKING THE UPPER MIDWEST
by Bruce Carlson .... paperback $7.95
101 WAYS FOR MIDWESTERNERS TO "DO IN" THEIR
NEIGHBOR'S PESKY DOG WITHOUT GETTING CAUGHT
by Bruce Carlson .... paperback $5.95

RIVER BOOKS

ON THE SHOULDERS OF A GIANT
by M. Cody and D. Walker .... paperback $9.95
SKUNK RIVER ANTHOLOGY
by Gene "Will" Olson .... paperback $9.95
JACK KING vs. DETECTIVE MACKENZIE
by Netha Bell .... paperback $9.95
LOST & BURIED TREASURES ALONG THE MISSISSIPPI
by Netha Bell & Gary Scholl .... paperback $9.95
MISSISSIPPI RIVER PO' FOLK
by Pat Wallace .... paperback $9.95
STRANGE FOLKS ALONG THE MISSISSIPPI
by Pat Wallace .... paperback $9.95
GHOSTS OF THE OHIO RIVER (from Pittsburgh to Cincinnati)
by Bruce Carlson .... paperback $9.95
GHOSTS OF THE OHIO RIVER (from Cincinnati to Louisville)
by Bruce Carlson .... paperback $9.95
GHOSTS OF THE MISSISSIPPI RIVER (Minneapolis to Dubuque)
by Bruce Carlson .... paperback $9.95
GHOSTS OF THE MISSISSIPPI RIVER (Dubuque to Keokuk)
by Bruce Carlson .... paperback $9.95
TALL TALES OF THE MISSISSIPPI RIVER
by Dan Titus .... paperback $9.95

TALL TALES OF THE MISSOURI RIVER
by Dan Titus .... paperback $9.95
RIVER SHARKS & SHENANIGANS
(tales of riverboat gambling of years ago)
by Netha Bell .... paperback $9.95
UNSOLVED MYSTERIES OF THE MISSISSIPPI
by Netha Bell .... paperback $9.95
TALES OF HACKETT'S CREEK (1940s Mississippi River kids)
by Dan Titus .... paperback $9.95
101 WAYS TO USE A DEAD RIVER FLY
by Bruce Carlson .... paperback $7.95
LET'S US GO DOWN TO THE RIVER 'N ...
by various authors .... paperback $9.95
LOST & BURIED TREASURE OF THE MISSOURI
by Netha Bell .... paperback $9.95

COOKBOOKS

ROARING 20's COOKBOOK
by Bruce Carlson .... paperback $11.95
DEPRESSION COOKBOOK
by Bruce Carlson .... paperback $11.95
LAKES COUNTRY COOKBOOK
by Bruce Carlson .... paperback $11.95
A COOKBOOK FOR THEM WHAT AIN'T DONE A LOT OF COOKIN'
by Bruce Carlson .... paperback $11.95
FLAT-OUT DIRT-CHEAP COOKIN' COOKBOOK
by Bruce Carlson .... paperback $11.95
APHRODISIAC COOKING
by Bruce Carlson .... paperback $11.95
WILD CRITTER COOKBOOK
by Bruce Carlson .... paperback $11.95
I GOT FUNNIER-THINGS-TO-DO-THAN-COOKIN' COOKBOOK
by Louise Lum .... paperback $11.95
MISSISSIPPI RIVER COOKIN' BOOK
by Bruce Carlson .... paperback $11.95
HUNTING IN THE NUDE COOKBOOK
by Bruce Carlson .... paperback $9.95
DAKOTA COOKIN'
by Bruce Carlson .... (3x5) paperback $5.95
IOWA COOKIN'
by Bruce Carlson .... (3x5) paperback $5.95

MICHIGAN COOKIN'
by Bruce Carlson .... (3x5) paperback $5.95
MINNESOTA COOKIN'
by Bruce Carlson .... (3x5) paperback $5.95
MISSOURI COOKIN'
by Bruce Carlson .... (3x5) paperback $5.95
ILLINOIS COOKIN'
by Bruce Carlson .... (3x5) paperback $5.95
WISCONSIN COOKIN'
by Bruce Carlson .... (3x5) paperback $5.95
HILL COUNTRY COOKIN'
by Bruce Carlson .... (3x5) paperback $5.95
MIDWEST SMALL TOWN COOKIN'
by Bruce Carlson .... (3x5) paperback $5.95
APHRODISIAC COOKIN'
by Bruce Carlson .... (3x5) paperback $5.95
PREGNANT LADY COOKIN'
by Bruce Carlson .... (3x5) paperback $5.95
GOOD COOKIN' FROM THE PLAIN PEOPLE
by Bruce Carlson .... (3x5) paperback $5.95
WORKING GIRL COOKING
by Bruce Carlson .... (3x5) paperback $5.95
COOKING FOR ONE
by Barb.Layton .... paperback $11.95
SUPER SIMPLE COOKING
by Barb Layton .... (3x5) paperback $5.95
OFF TO COLLEGE COOKBOOK
by Barb Layton .... (3x5) paperback $5.95
COOKING WITH THINGS THAT GO SPLASH
by Bruce Carlson .... (3x5) paperback $5.95
COOKING WITH THINGS THAT GO MOO
by Bruce Carlson .... (3x5) paperback $5.95
COOKING WITH SPIRITS
by Bruce Carlson .... (3x5) paperback $5.95
INDIAN COOKING COOKBOOK
by Bruce Carlson .... paperback $9.95
DIAL-A-DREAM COOKBOOK
by Bruce Carlson .... (3x5) paperback $5.95
HORMONE HELPER COOKBOOK .... (3x5) paperback $5.95

MISCELLANEOUS BOOKS

DEAR TABBY (letters to and from a feline advice columnist)
     by Bruce Carlson .... paperback $5.95
HOW TO BEHAVE (etiquette advice for non-traditional
and awkward circumstances such as attending dogfights,
what to do when your blind date turns out to be your spouse, etc.)
     by Bruce Carlson .... paperback $5.95
REVENGE OF THE ROADKILL
     by Bruce Carlson .... paperback $7.95